EMBED WITH GAMES

EMBED WITH GAMES

A Year on the Couch with Game Developers

Cara Ellison

First published in Great Britain in 2015 by Polygon Books,
an imprint of Birlinn Ltd.

West Newington House
10 Newington Road
Edinburgh
EH9 1QS

www.polygonbooks.co.uk

A CIP catalogue reference for this book is available from
the British Library.

ISBN 978 1 84697 344 4
eISBN 978 0 85790 889 6

Typeset by Freight in Brown and Poynter
Printed and bound in Great Britain by
TJ International Ltd, Padstow, Cornwall

Contents

Foreword by Kieron Gillen

Foreword
Kieron Gillen

I met Cara three times in the year she was travelling.

The first time was in New York. She was there, working on this. I'd been there meeting my corporate paymasters at Marvel, and was waiting for a car to the airport and had time to grab a drink beforehand. Cara was late, so she joined me in the car for the hour drive to the airport. We spent the journey giggling like teenagers, telling awful stories about awful people. She mainly said how much she liked The Weeknd's 'Often' because 'he likes to do it, often'. As I boarded the train and she got a train back into New York, I felt assured she was fine and the adventures were good for her.

The second time was at Nine Worlds convention, at one of the asteroid hotels orbiting Heathrow. You get that close to an airport, and time and space warps. You are not in Britain any more. You are in a Ballardian land, a liminal space. Cara looked wan. I dragged her to the expensive hotel restaurant and fed her steak, then stole the red wine to take to the fireside conversation panel we were meant to be doing. We were both tense and tired, rowed a little, and I left worried about her.

The third time was near the end, in a basement flat in Brighton. She was passing through on one of her journeys, and had arranged a night of boardgames, which basically turned into a load of us doing Rock Band at 3 a.m., like everyone was back in 2010 again. She seemed tired and strained, and disappointed. She had done so much, but wanted to do so much more and felt that it was impossible. I left on the train, glad that her adventures were nearly over, and hoped that whatever came next would be kinder.

What came next was Cara deciding to step away from games writing. Well, at least that'll be kinder.

I've worried about her a lot this year. To be fair, I've worried about *everyone* in games this year, but Cara more than most. There is a psychic strain to playing videogames for a living, which is little to do with the work and more to do with the sense of vocation to it. If you don't care, and you don't mind the lack of money, you can amble along, playing games you like, writing some just-enough copy, and then go home and do whatever it is you like doing.

The problem comes when you actually care about games in a way above and beyond just liking them. You can double that problem if you actually care about the craft of writing too, because then you end up wrestling with all the problems in the industry. And trust me – if you care about games in that sense that you feel they're capital-I important, you eventually come to care about writing too. You learn to care about the writing because working out ways to communicate that napalm in your head as effectively as you can is about all that's keeping you together.

Games writers are writers and writers are fuck-ups. We wouldn't do this if we had any sense. It is, to quote someone Cara hates, the hardest way to earn an easy living.

I write that in part to have a little whine, but in part to give a context to what Cara Ellison of Aberdeen has done for you lot. This is an emotionally punishing job anyway, especially if you do the sort of open-ribcage writing Cara does. She'd have been exhausted and broken at the end of 2014 even if she had a staff job somewhere. Instead, she decided to start a Patreon and use it to fund her travelling the world, to give a global portrait of the games industry, the people in it, what they do and why.

This obviously sounds like a lot of fun. Wait till you read the book. It ends up not being that much fun at all. It ends up feeling even masochistic. By halfway through, I was hoping that Cara just went home. By the end, I was hoping Cara found a home to go home to. I pictured her as a pillar-box red square in an existential platform game, CARA ELLISON WAS ALONE.

Luckily for us, we didn't have to do it, and we just get to see the results. As a whole, in its *Rashomon* structure, it ends up being a snapshot of the games industry in 2014, from the top to the bottom. Delete everything in that last sentence after the comma. There is no 'top' or 'bottom' here – this is game development as a rainforest. These are a dozen ecological niches being filled, with Cara as our hair-dyed cyberpunk Attenborough bringing us footage. When the media still gives us one idea of what games are like, those sterile glass fortresses of Electronic Arts, this is a kaleidoscope. As a gonzoid apostle of Thompson, Cara is as much of a character in it as anyone else. If I wanted to create a time capsule to show what it was like to live through This Turbulent Year in games, I may give you this. This is what it was like for us, guys. Learn. It was awesome and terrible, and it was the future being born, red and screaming.

Cara's also lucky. I'm from an older generation of games writer. I joined early enough to catch the tail end of the decadent 1990s and left at the peak of the first indie boom circa 2010. I've got a bunch of anecdotes from the time, but one dates from around 2000. I find myself in a social situation with a developer from Looking Glass, specifically someone who'd just worked on *Thief II*. All things Immersive Sim are basically my speciality at the time. I float a theory – namely, that I look at Looking Glass a little like The Velvet Underground were to the 1960s, in terms of power vs influence vs sales. It's my sort of theory. They don't blink. They passionately agree. That's absolutely what they are.

There's two reasons for telling that anecdote. First, the wonder when meeting people who believe in games just as intensely as you do. *Oh. You're not wrong. I'm not alone in this.* Second, that I was surprised at all at that happening, or thought it worth remembering. *Because something like that happens to Cara on every second page.*

I read this book and felt jealous of Cara, wishing I had a chance to do anything as audacious in scope as this. Yes, she's sundered herself from her emotional support groups and any sense of permanence, but the results speak for themselves.

If Cara never writes about games again, it will be a huge loss. If Cara never writes about games again, these 50,000 or so words are a worthy monument.

Kotaku once sorta said that Kieron Gillen invented Games Journalism, which still makes him laugh. He first wrote about games in the Byzantine period of Amiga Power, was full-time for PC Gamer in its Imperial Phase and left games writing after founding the Viking Tribe of Rock, Paper, Shotgun. When he decided to earn some money, he started writing comics, which he presently does for Marvel, Image and Avatar Press. He's also the Father of New Gam ('Don't Mention The War' – Ed.) He lives in South London. He still hates Zelda.

Embed with ...

Embed with ...
London

My friends George Buckenham and Alice O'Connor kindly agreed to be written about as an introduction to my 'embedding' with strangers. George has been making games for years, both traditional and non-traditional; the central focus is on his outlook on games as a whole. Alice is Senior Editor for Shacknews but has more recently done design work for the sadly now disbanded Hide&Seek. They happen to live in the same flat. Both are heavily involved in setting up renowned London games and music event The Wild Rumpus. This details my week with them and the lead-up to the event. All beautiful photographs of The Wild Rumpus were taken by Robin Baumgarten. The rest were taken, badly, by me.

London

There are two sleeping monsters to kill before I leave the craggy beaten shores of Great Britain: one I love, and one I hate. The nearest convenient colossus is an hour away by train, looming in the darkness like a knobbled old fuckwit, grinding up all the talented people like Sarlacc. London.

When I first arrived in London two years ago I was a blonde. By the time I left, I was a brunette, limping under a weight of self-esteem strangulation, a crooked diet and caustic personal struggles. The filthy drizzle-smeared veins of train lines had, in the end, drowned ambition, punched the colour from my hair. Making my way back into the steepled January murk again, like a pilgrimage into Mordor, the train's gentle lull lies to me about how I should feel about it. Looming shadows lean over the train as it pulls in to London Bridge, a grand kind of arrogance. New York's welcome is a fast-talking, loud, PAY-ATTENTION-TO-ME one, but

London lies on an expensive chaise longue and slow-waits until you notice that everything is controlled by him, and fuck you, because here you are again.

Hated London. Polluted, angry, alcoholic London. I'm going to kill it this time. Slice, *chiburi, noto tsuke*, done. I listen to the Rolling Stones' 'Doom And Gloom' as I clamber through the train. This bag's big enough for three changes of clothes, a laptop, and all of the stupid cables I intend to strangle London with. You defeated me last time, London. This time: Hundred Rending Legs. No mercy. Like Voldo's foot to your neck. Finished.

Worn at the end of a year of trying to think of pitches and wishing there was more scope and time for ambition in the games press, I'd finally pitched people on the internet the idea of embedded games journalism, an idea had over a number of months before and threatened on Twitter like a surreal dream until I ended up drunk and frustrated in a friend's spare room with a Patreon page open in front of me.

That room was to be occupied by a baby soon. Somehow in life I am always the single friend surrounded by couples and children, but though long-term singledom may leave room for the kind of insecurity where you imagine your corpse not being discovered for months and no ever-present friend to argue down your self-hatred, what it does give you is zero responsibilities, no sense of shame, no reason to deny spontaneity, no reason to come home, room to make your life uncomfortable, an unrelenting belief that even if no one loves you enough to be with you, the whole world can be your boyfriend instead. And the world did want to be my patron at least: five hundred people signed up to pay my monthly cross-world flights to game developers so I could write about their worlds and immediately made me homeless that January. (Part of me resented that, almost, as if people were paying to see the spectacle of my discomfort, but the entire thing was my idea, and people warn you about going on the internet drunk, and I didn't listen.)

As I arrive in London, I am entirely vagabond with nothing to lose except a bag of clothes, a laptop, and the respect of the entire games industry, nay internet, if I fuck all of this stupid idea up. The stakes are very high, and the threat of my first post to my subscribers making everyone unsubscribe feels like a knife held very close to my neck at night, so close that it is possible to feel the notches of it imprint on my oesophagus in the dead of night.

Stepney Green's tube station is a quaint empty Victorian affair, all criss-cross wrought iron over pale green and white tiles, just as it would have been in 1901 when it opened. I walk, Elder Scrolls emburdened, up the steps on a well-worn walk to flatmates George Buckenham and Alice O'Connor's place, in a 1960s concrete maisonette. I've always hated the word 'maisonette'. It conjures up images of a Cold War-poster French housewife in a checked pinny, pastel walls. This is not what it is.

But because like the rest of the city East London 'got fucked in the war' (Alice), this area is home to a patchwork of looks. *The Wire*'s inner-city Baltimore combines an eternal fight between talented young poor people who have painted everything with fluorescent colour and burritos, Nathan Barley yuppies who want things to be chrome, and the multitude of accents of the families and students coming to seek a London fortune.

London Indies

George and Alice live in their respective rooms in the rented maisonette with a third new flatmate, Tef, near a Stepney Fried Chicken takeout and 'a pub that sells nice pies' (Alice). They are part of a group of small developers who support each other here in London, through little gestures and monthly pub outings under the informal label of 'London Indies'. The London Indies discuss builds of games, eat packets of crisps and share ideas. I have a fascination with their gentle concern for each other: for me London's hostile living conditions are completely at odds with the way the small developers treat each other here. Familiar faces often turn up at London Indies such as Ed Key of <u>Proteus</u>, <u>Alex May</u> of Eufloria, <u>Ricky Haggett</u> and <u>Dick Hogg</u> – many others often stop by to discuss things and show and test games. I am recently aware this group has developed a taste for gourmet burgers. This last thing is the fault of the newly London-installed Terry Cavanagh, primarily famous for his punishing games VVVVVV and Super Hexagon. The London Indies cheerfully soldier on in spite of the oppressive expense of living in the world's most costly city.

George answers the door: he's got these beautiful long black eyelashes and clear pretty white skin so that he always looks about twenty when he's actually twenty-six. 'I'm not looking forward to getting older,' he says, 'because then I can't annoy people this way. I could have been doing this way younger ... I mean, look at Rami [Ismail, of Vlambeer], Droqen [maker of Starseed Pilgrim].' Both of these developers are in their early twenties, and I tell him about William Pugh, developer on the successful The Stanley Parable, who is a bastard nineteen years old.

Inside the flat is cramped, chilly. It has one of those old fireplaces with wheatsheaf patterns on it, now flaking white paint; screwdrivers and cardboard boxes populate the flat. This is a flat that makes every kind of game, not just the ones that sit on a computer screen.

Journalistic Integrity

I am declaring right now for journalistic integrity, as I write on my third day in Stepney Green, that I have drunk at least ten cups of tea and about six gin and tonics, all supplied by Alice and George. Last night I played Netrunner with George until 2 a.m., the *Tron: Legacy* soundtrack undulating through rectangular slices of cyberpunk nostalgia. I lost as Corp, won as Runner. All the while, Maddy the cat made a squeaking noise sleeping in a cardboard box. One time she came up and sneezed on me and went away again. Maybe the cat is allergic to me. Perhaps that is why it is sleeping in a cardboard box. I am eating antihistamines.

It is freezing in the flat, so most of the time we wear

jumpers and think about hot food, and I try to type and sell interesting stuff. I have been on both BBC Radio Five Live and Resonance FM talking in a terrified manner about Patreon. Alice has been kindly letting me sleep in a single bed with her in her (very) small room. We have not yet spooned.

*

Alice is tall, knowing, an Essex girl with blue hair and a grin like a Cheshire cat. Probably the kindest person I know, she also has a certain deliberation about her, like she is always sure of things. I have told Alice I think that the mouldy bathroom with an interesting variety of lagan and hair products is the centrepiece of her Stepney flat. On Saturday night Alice and I stopped to stare at the local old man pub, The Horn of Plenty, while it vibrated the entire neighbourhood with shit pop hit 'Blurred Lines' and flashed orange lights. George has worn his 868-HACK T-shirt from Michael Brough two days in a row and I have pointed this out and he has changed it. Over some gin and some tea, George has told me his life story, and his feelings on London.

Sparks & Glamour

'I came into games not because I loved games, but because they were a really good example of ... the intersection between people and technology,' George tells me. 'How people work with machines. How machines can pretend to be humans. AI, HCI. I did a bunch of stuff on visual systems. Trying to imitate animals: write code that can navigate the same way animals do. Most HCI is reasonably boring if you look at it, and then you look at games, games are fucking... That's basically all it is. HCIs. Human Computer Interaction.' George is fiddling with some sort of plastic tiling toy where the tiles slot into each other like Tetris.

George is just as kind as Alice, in a shyer, more contemplative way. He and I met at Rock Paper Shotgun drinks two years ago when Alice tried to get me to proposition him after rounds of awful tequila. At the time, I needed a place to live in London, and Alice was quite sure moving in with a boy was the best way to attain a cheap (free) rental. The Sexual Favours move. I didn't end up propositioning George, but I always wondered if he'd overheard this drunken babble. Instead of propositioning him we just hung out over the next few years; I slowly realised that George is this background magician. A sort of stealth games operative. He's at every event, everywhere, quietly orchestrating his secret games projects like an amiable, screwdriver-wielding Sam Fisher.

George got a Cognitive Science MA from the University of Edinburgh in 2009 which he says was 'half AI, half psychology' and that it was necessary to learn how to code during that time. He made Hell Is Other People because he was impatient to make games, and moved to London to be with friends he missed after graduating. He started a job at a telecoms company, and visited a lot of Cambridge game jams, where he made the prototype for his game CUBES, which would eventually be released on iOS in 2012. He befriended Alice at London Indies. He got a job as Technical Lead at PLA Studios in March 2011, doing work for hire projects like get182.com (for Blink-182) and Fantasea (for Azealia Banks). George now works for Die Gute Fabrik, makers of Johann Sebastian Joust, programming an adventure exploration game called <u>Mutazione</u>. This is his day job; much of my time will be spent peeking over his shoulder at the beautiful scenery in the Unity engine's window.

'Do you think that's the draw of video games?' I ask. 'The lights. The sparks. The glamour of it?'

'Yeah, totally,' he says, lying on the couch like I'm a therapist. As soon as I have this thought I feel a bit fucked up. 'It's the same thing when I was young,' he muses. 'I remember being really excited when you can press the Enter key and suddenly the screen does all this crazy stuff and you made that happen. As part of my dissertation I ended up making an amazingly complicated bit of machinery unnecessarily complicated. But I ended up being able to go to the command line and press a button and some lights would turn on. And then I could go to the command line and press a button and those lights would turn off. And when I got that working I spent about twenty minutes turning the lights on and off and going "This is amazing! Amazing!"'

George is adamant that though he had an Amstrad in his house when he was growing up, it's not the thing that made him a programmer or made him want to make games. This seems in contrast to all those Silicon Valley brogrammer types who always claim programming talent is funnelled through childhood or the stereotype that the makers of games were making games as soon as they could work a computer. It seems as if what makes George want to be involved in games now is that it enables him to experiment with what he's interested in.

There's always this latent feeling in the games industry that we should be serving the games, but I get the very strong feeling that games serve George. He makes them serve his own curiosities and then puts them in the world to observe how people interact with them. This is probably why his work is so often unconventional: George developed a game last year called Punch The Custard, where you get two bowls of custard hooked up to a circuit, and two players literally just punch into the bowl of custard over and over to see which person can do it fastest.

The score is displayed via a monitor. I saw it in action at Gamecity, and it was hilarious to watch as well as to play. It looks extremely rude. It's a spectacle. He says he thought of the title first and worked from there. Of course he did.

The Wild Rumpus

It was in August 2011 in a glamorous Nandos (a sordid middle-class chicken hut chain where every dish tastes like cayenne pepper dissolved in lemon juice) that George says he was asked to help form a committee to hold something called The Wild Rumpus. The Wild Rumpus is game roughhousing: the informal event takes place in a hired bar, features simple lo-fi multiplayer games you can play with friends between drinks. They use projectors and huge screens, and the games are always visually mesmerising, competitively thrilling, or require players to engage in social theatre lubricated by beer. It's always busy, and there is as much pleasure in spectating the bright colours and social friction that the games bring as there is in actually playing games there. 'Closer in spirit to party, playground, or even drinking games, these are all games that you can't play at home on your own,' it is declared. The atmosphere is in between that of a game night with friends and an electro-pop club night with extremely well-behaved patrons.

The Splintercade at The Wild Rumpus, the result of Alice's labours

When I ask George what the intention is when he makes games he says it depends on what sort of game he's making. For Mutazione, he says the intention is to delight the player via an intersection of magical vistas, ethereal music and narrative elements. With his own work, he wants to experiment on the player, be surprised by their reactions. With The Wild Rumpus, it's all about the spectating. People come off the street to see the games being played there, he told me one morning. 'And if they go away without ever having played one of the games, that's okay,' he says.

Since George's First Great Nandos Proposition there have been nine successful Wild Rumpus events and they attract people who have never played games as well as those who make and play them. George and Alice both contribute their DIY talents to organising these events, while Marie Foulston has moved to Toronto to continue orchestrating operations from abroad. Richard Hogg, Ricky Haggett and Pat Ashe assist in organising from England. George helped build The Beast, an arcade cabinet that has housed any number of original arcade games, and he and Alice also made the custom joypads for Tenya Wanya Teens, a game that requires a whole bank of the joypad's buttons to flash different colours throughout the game. Both are things of beauty.

George and The Beast

This week is the run-up to the tenth Wild Rumpus. Alice tells me she's been stealing abandoned wooden palettes from streets to paint for the Wild Rumpus Splintercade. They are stacked on their balcony next to an ashtray with a mound of cigarettes in it.

'One's pretty filthy,' she says, pulling at her cropped hair with a half-grin as she regards the palettes. 'It'll take too much work to clean it up. I'll have to go and find another one.' A few days later, pretty much everything in the flat is covered in blue paint, including Alice's arms and desk, and there is a saw hazardously abandoned in the middle of the living-room floor; I blunder over it while gathering laptop cables. Gladly I survive with all limbs intact.

Mutazione and Die Gute Fabrik

I ask George if he'd quit work on Mutazione to work for a big studio. 'I'd rather not work in games than get paid badly and also work really hard on stuff that I don't own,' he says. His experience working in programming beyond games has hugely affected how he thinks about work inside the games industry. 'Getting paid less than I would working outside of games doing a similar thing' is not something he says he's keen on. 'I'm kind of itching to expand outside of games. I really want to do VJing. People who do graphics for live shows. I'm doing a whole bunch of stuff with graphics and I find that really interesting.'

*

As I sit here, the proposed soundtrack for Mutazione is echoing gently around the room. The sounds of glockenspiel notes and bells are otherworldly, making me feel calm and less allergic to the cat, who is a catnip junkie rolling around on the floor.

Kay, the main character in Mutazione, is this little 2D girl on-screen. She seems friendly but expressionless, walking from one screen to the other past neon-lit buildings. There is a strong sense of place in the game, as if Kay were negotiating dreamworlds become tangible. George regularly Skypes the rest of the Gute Fabrik team across the world: Nils Deneken in Copenhagen, Douglas Wilson in New York, and Alessandro Coronas in Sardinia. I listened to their debates one afternoon: should they polish now, or after the story elements have been put in place? Should they get the time of day lighting working before putting in story elements? What state should the game be in before submitting the build to show investors? Doug reminds the team the transitions have to be smooth to make it pleasant to play. Afterwards, I ask George if working remotely is difficult. Does he wish they were in an office together? The answer is yes: sometimes it's difficult to show the team what has been added and how if they're not there in front of your monitor. Instead, text and screenshots are all they go on. But office space and visas are expensive, and the internet makes everything possible. George gets to work on this as well as fiddling around with monitor splitter cables for London games events.

Fucking Party

We are invited to go to Terry Cavanagh's new flat in Aldgate for his thirtieth birthday. As we leave, Alice says to George, 'I saw a Christmas tree on one end of Cephas Street, and a Christmas tree stand on the other end, you know. The tree might be too dead to use though.' Apparently they are planning on nicking those as well. I ask why. 'For Christmas,' Alice says. (It is a month after Christmas.) What the fuck are they going to use a dead Christmas tree for? Days later I ask her what she was going to do with it. 'Something,' she says. 'Maybe The Wild Rumpus. I hadn't thought that far ahead.'

Terry's new flat in Aldgate requires one to go through huge glass doors and take the lift up six floors; inside, the corridors resemble a pinewood-doored hotel. It's the first time, I think, in the UK, that I've ever been in a stairwell that didn't resemble murky hundred-year-old dungeon steps (they are our speciality), and the first time I've ever been in an apartment building in London that has a concierge. Part of me wants to ask the concierge about the weirdest thing he's ever seen happen in the building, but I doubt he'd be able to tell me, and frankly I look like the sort of flotsam that Terry might end up getting chucked out of the flat for.

Terry Cavanagh is the sort of person everyone wishes they were: prolific, talented, modest, gentle, soft-spoken, slightly mischievous when drunk. Though it would make him blush to hear it, he is always thought of fondly. The first time I ever really spoke to him was in a goth-rock bar last year in San Francisco at 3 a.m., where we bought overpriced slices of pizza and attempted to find the mysterious melodious Jenn Frank, who is the voice of Terry's game Super Hexagon. Recently Terry's years of work putting out game after game has paid off. It's enabled him to move to the aforementioned most expensive city in the world, and his long-time co-conspirator Stephen Lavelle, aka Increpare, has also moved in with him here. If you put both of their games end to end, you could probably reach the sun.

I bring Terry hexagon-shaped chocolates, and Terry confesses he is ill. He is drinking tea and looks extremely infectious. I delight in Stephen showing me around the flat – Terry and he are both curiously proud of their closet, in which they have put what looks like a year's supply of toilet roll. I didn't know that Terry played the guitar, but there are at least two sitting in his room, and Stephen tells me Terry plays the accordion too. Stephen shows me the bathroom, and his proud stash of German shower gels (bulk ordered), Speick Natural Deo Dusch. There are at least six bottles of it in a line in the bathroom. It smells like Man.

*

Alex May is at the party. He makes me a margarita and tells me about his new game: it's a procedural game about growing trees. I hold back on making a Eufloria 'off-shoot' joke. I tell him I think we're on the brink of a bedroom coding revival like in the Spectrum days: small developers reinvesting money in each other, and supporting each other, like Cliffski funding Mitu Khandaker-Kokoris's <u>Redshirt</u>. He agrees; he thinks it's an exciting time to be around. I talk to Holly Gramazio, a producer on Tiny Games, who has recently gone freelance after Hide&Seek's closure.

Holly talks about the Arts Council's interest in games. She wants me to write about the events she'll put on. Meanwhile, Terry has received a giant chocolate birthday cake. There is a unanimous decision amongst the attendees that he should headbutt it. He does so; chocolate chips fly everywhere. Later, he will punch the cake, and it will fragment across the floor. I have it on good authority some impish guests goaded him into it.

I am on the balcony with Increpare, whose game Slave of God is one of the most profound games I've ever played. The air is on frost edge. London is too bright to show us stars in the sky, but the balcony overlooks an old Victorian factory, and over to the right, the lights of Canary Wharf are almost a good enough substitute for constellations.

I remember the first time I looked out over Canary Wharf's jagged lines pocked with white; it reminds me of M83 and being stiflingly heartbroken. I do not like this city very much, I think, but I love that these people can exist in it. I love that they are making things. London tries so hard to prevent it. But people are making things.

Back inside RedEye Ste Curran sternly gives me tax advice: 'I know you won't listen to me' (I think about listening to him), and then we decide to go out to a bar. The night gets blurry here: it ends with my being in a kebab shop with Terry and George, and the next morning I awake in Alice's bed fully clothed with no glasses on and a curious taste of old chicken in my mouth.

Casualties of Journalism

It's Thursday. I've lost my glasses, I'm hungover. I've been here for five days. I suspect Maddy the cat has slept on my head at least once. My throat feels like it's swelling up and my eyes constantly water. We are running out of Piriton. Maddy came and sat on me once on the couch; I sneezed very loudly on her and she ran away. This, my friends, is how you get revenge on cats.

Alice has spooned me. I was the small spoon. Alice has also secretly been feeding me vegan food, and I begin to suspect this has weakened my immune system to let the cat germs in. Alice may be trying to kill me. I think I might have contracted Terry's flu. George tells me they are going to have International Karate at The Wild Rumpus. In my drug-addled, histamine-lined brain this seems unlikely.

Without my glasses George has begun to resemble Joseph Gordon-Levitt and I have to write about a sex game for RPS. George has asked me at least three more times to play Netrunner with him. By Friday I would escape to a Bethnal Green café to de-cat, and then find Alice'd sent me to a vegan café. Part of me wonders if I will leave the flat alive. But outside the shelter of the flat where my friends live, London grinds away as if it knows I am coming for it. As if it knows I am trying to find its secrets. It has one last blow to strike against me.

The Energy to Hate

It's 1 a.m., the night before my last day, and I am walking home by myself across East London. The black air around me is frostbitten; I can see my own breath billow out in big curls of white mist as I walk quiet pavements. 'Young Blood' by The Naked and Famous is playing in my ears. No one is around but a fox, who stops to look at me by a grass verge, like they used to in New Cross.

Frostcold tears happen. I cry them silently all the way to Globe Road. I remember London. I remember when my home was here.

London was the first time I cried like adult women cry. Before London I'd never been sad. Before London I'd been in love, I'd been heartbroken, I'd been lonely, I'd been broke, I'd been horny and hungry and ambitious and frustrated and outraged and annoyed and even hypothermic close-to-gone. But London was the first time I'd ever really cried like

I could cry my soul into death. In London, I cried in front of all of my heroes. Once, I cried for thirty minutes in front of Kieron Gillen, a writer and friend, who had somewhere else to be, and it is the most embarrassing memory I'll ever have. To be that crippled in front of someone you want to be invincible to. To be that humiliated is really an achievement. Living in London was like walking through a pitch-black tunnel, a crowbar in hand, bludgeoning whatever attacked, reading the echoes on corpses to find the exit. It was Half-Life overgrown and horrifying. I was disorientated when I left, and only now do I understand I am in the sort of dark that is *outside*.

But there's one thing that I understand, and it is that when all those emotional vertebrae broke and reformed they had a different quality. They began to have a word-making, listen-to-me quality. They began to know they were worth more. They began to need company. They began to make money. They began to trip switches. My metabolism, where before it was based in asking, is now based in fuck you. Where before it ran on agreement, it's now run on sharpened revenge. You can be sure, London, that I do not agree. And I will never agree again. London's cruel breaking of me is a metal coating. Crying in front of your heroes is a sort of invincibility. This will be the last time I will find the energy to hate London. You can stand up and never sit down.

The Night of The Wild Rumpus

I awake to the sound of The Blitz; Alice and George have already gone to the set-up at BL-NK, and next door are enacting some sort of bombardment to wake me. I tiptoe downstairs: the blue and orange-painted palettes are gone. But the paint splotches all over the flat remain.

A feeling of quiet dread and sadness comes over me. Last night Alice told me something as I climbed over her to occupy my space; the space between her and the wall in the early morning witching. This is the only place that has ever felt like home to her. She used to sleep in a room that was a throughway for the rest of her family, no door, feeling like she was intruding on others' space constantly. This is the only place where she's felt like she belonged. Where she is now creating things that make her happy.

She told me that she loves feeling useful in a practical way; writing video game news on the intangible internet for five years has made her crave physically helping others. She is excited by the prospect of being needed, and of making things. I lay transfixed by the wall and her body, my own smile and her happiness, hugging myself.

As I make some grey coffee I muse that tonight Alice will have her hands full as the bar empties of beer, the game cables will dislodge, and the DJ sets swap over. George and Alice aren't getting paid to do it; it's just a labour of love, and a bonus if they break even. Marie Foulston teeters over emails in Toronto, like an anxious mother. Ricky Haggett and Pat Ashe will be working hard too, their ever-present optimism lapping at the edges where the cables connect.

Days later I would ask George: in those late hours in our first alcoholic acquaintance, when Alice was loudly suggesting I proposition you, if I had asked, if I had asked, would you have said yes?

'Probably,' he says.

Probably. But I wasn't the sort to ask then. I am now, but London is over tonight.

In the evening, I zip up my boots to guard against the grey crags, arch trees, and everlasting dragons. I put extra layers on. The clasp on my bra feels rigid in the middle of my back, like a harness. I put warpaint on.

Outside, it's baltic. I couldn't eat anything before I left. My eyes won't stop watering. I know now: Terry has made me ill. London cackles through the rustle of the trees as I try to gather myself.

I can hear the music far away. The BL-NK building is a concrete doorstop in Shoreditch's hysterical throat.

I walk into the party, hands in pockets against the chill. I've taken whatever pills I could find in the flat hoping they weren't cat medicine. I've nothing in my stomach; I feel light-headed. My glasses are still lost and so my vision blurs after a few metres; the music gently beats and flashes neon greens and reds through the doorway and I walk towards it in a daydream.

Tom is playing a set.

Nidhogg, a two-player liquid-fast fencing simulator crams everyone towards its neon flesh. All night, people will fight for the controller and eat its feedback candy. Sugar of the most incredible reward. A tussle between strangers that feels more like an argument with someone before you fuck. Like both characters are Humphrey Bogart and Lauren Bacall, and the directors had given them foils and a two-hour drunk.

George and I tested it together this week, his fingers more used to the laptop controls, deftly stabbing me in the neck. But his beleaguered laptop, in the shadows of the London flat, struggled to allocate memory to the game. As I pressed to push my character into the air, sword arm outstretched, the laptop bucked and protested; the game slowed my avatar's arm to George's avatar. It seemed purposeful, balletic. The avatar slowed and slowed, and I thought I'd never seen anything as beautiful as this ugly orange silhouette, his jagged outline trip-falling towards his adored enemy, foil upheld, expectant. And then fast, it sped up, and we flung our weapons, picked them up, punched and retrieved and ran and lunged-to-the-head. It was the only kind of Nidhogg.

The LHS bikeshed, a spaceship simulator in a repurposed caravan.
Get through the gates or everyone dies. Everyone.

The Final Stage

And in the middle of the fray, I find beer. I am surrounded by the UK's most incisive game makers. I gather the troops to slay the dragon.

George wants to experiment on the player. I want to know about the player. I want to know what the intention is. What do you want to do? Do you want to move them, excite them, anguish them? Do you want to entrance them? Do you want to trap them and keep them and fuck them over? First, Terry Cavanagh. I ask him what his intention is. 'With every game it's different,' he says, 'but with Super Hexagon, I wanted them to be put in a trance state.' He wanted them to be mesmerised, put in the zone. He wanted them to be caught in the moving lines.

Mitu Khandaker-Kokoris of Redshirt says she looks for two things: first, 'delight', and second, 'satire'. George Khandaker-Kokoris, her husband beside her, is also a game designer. I ask him what he looks for. 'I want awe,' he says. 'And design that makes people laugh.' I smile. They are married. They are two people who are similar, but are not the same. They overlap, but just enough.

Holly Gramazio, someone with more experience with real-world games, analogue games, tells me that she thinks of what action she wants the players to perform, and works backwards. She is the opposite of George: she thinks of an enjoyable or silly performance or spectacle, and reverse engineers it. George makes something experimental to almost record what sort of reaction is made – Holly knows the outcome, and structures her games appropriately.

But the most beautiful insight of the night comes from a late-night, shouted conversation between Tom Armitage and me. He has just finished DJing his set. 'It's that old thing,' he tells me, squinting at his own thought-process, sweating beer in hand. 'That old Volkswagen Beetle thing. At first glance, you see a curve. On second glance, you see three curves.' He gestures three humps. 'On last glance, you see the details.'

He elaborates: FPSs are easy to sell to a player. On first glance, you see the beautiful vistas. The visual opportunities it opens to you. On second glance, you understand the systems in place (in FPSs, the ability to shoot someone). On third glance, you see the small details; the depth. And often, FPSs are short on that last thing. 'You want to get all three right,' he says. Some players look for one of the glances over the others. Some designers design for only one of those glances. Tom says he wants to design for all three.

Super Pinata Pro counts up candy in the background; Kozilek jumps up and down to Luftrausers. That's it. That's the final piece.

Tom hugs me goodbye. We promise to see each other more often for drinks.

The party is finishing up. Alice, George, Ricky and Pat are cleaning up, I am swept away by the plans for the afterparty, where my body collapses, ill and exhausted, into orange juice. In the morning, when I get up, George isn't around. Alice takes me for brunch, but, as fate would have it, we end up in a Nandos. It is Alice's first one. She says she was pleased with how The Wild Rumpus went. Nothing went wrong, although they didn't show International Karate +, and The Beast was out of commission. George and her did good. The whole team did good. It was one of the biggest and best. She asks me if I'm excited to be leaving, and I say I'm afraid. But I will miss her. It was the best of times, it was the worst of times. I had to kill London. But I did it. I feel like London is now just a blip on a world map. Edinburgh, my second, more beloved nemesis, waits on the scroll. STAGE CLEARED.

Drinking in bars
with Karla Zimonja

Gone Home developer Karla Zimonja is yelling at me over a glass of rosé wine in a woozy backstreet diner, the kind where everyone spits their late-night accounting frustrations over foods so greasy they stain wooden tables.

This month, I have been a passenger through Northern England and London while preparing to leave. This is a mostly meditative post; if it seems to lack the spirit of the last it is because it's not really a piece of 'embedded journalism': this will begin earnestly next month. I have been preparing to leave, giving away my room to a new tenant, giving away my clothes, applying for press visas. Karla Zimonja, co-founder of The Fullbright Company and co-creator of the multi-award-winning game Gone Home came to visit the UK to give a talk, and our time together was rushed between meetings, events, friends, storms and floods. But there was still time to talk about women's nefarious agendas.

The Little Sisters of Bioshock can either be cured and made pure, or killed and harvested.

There's a fear that lives in women, and it's the fear that we are not normal. Stories are usually written by men and women about men; because it's normal to think men are interesting, they can be both hypocritical and heroic. Though films like Young Adult do exist where the narrative follows a woman who is fundamentally broken yet headstrong, they are few. It's thought that women cannot be versatile: we are either beautiful or disgusting. Madonna/whore. When women are uncouth or anti-establishment, we are not celebrated, we are abhorred. When we are not pretty we are useless. When we don't care we are dangerous. Stories do this to us. Stories that talk about us as if we are an image and not people.

Gone Home, a game with narrative written by Steve Gaynor and edited by Karla Zimonja, is different. It is a game that has no bodies in it. It's just an environment, one that happens to be a 3D house. There are pictures of people – though very few. We get a glimpse of how Kaitlin and Sam Greenbriar look from their family portrait. But there are no non-player characters in the Gone Home house. Our own player character's body is weightless, invisible. It is part of the reason that it initially feels so uncomfortable there: there is an absence of physical bodies within the game, and to us, that is all women are. They are physical bodies. They are 3D objects we look at; they are usually not the narrative in our heads. They are not the Hemingways or the Chaucers. Women rarely get their narratives canonised. Women are usually not in charge of their own stories, and when they are, they are ignored, because they are not canon.

Gone Home didn't have the budget for 3D rigged women, which is the argument big budget studios also give for not including women characters. But Gone Home didn't include men's bodies either. The Fullbright Company designed to make people real without having to consider the one constraint that consistently objectifies and dehumanises women: the gaze of the player and a fixation on bodies.

Instead the discourse is given wholesale to women in direct contradiction to what usually happens. The first narrative discourse Gone Home indulges is to have one young woman leave another a note, seasoned with a kick of emotion, on the front door. The second is to have Sam's calm voice speak to you via audio diary. And suddenly, in your head, these young women are not invisible any more in the storm. They become people who are just like you.

*

'Steve doesn't have an "agenda",' she says on half-sleep. 'I HAVE A FUCKING "AGENDA". I want to help even out some of the inequality.'

I can't remember if she hit the table then; if she didn't let's just say she did. But I sat there thinking I was witnessing the terrible and wonderful.

'I HAVE A FUCKING "AGENDA".'

It felt like she'd reached into my body and plucked out a giant, sticky ball of elastic bands from my body, and with it all the tension of the past few years. I have a fucking agenda, I said silently over and over to myself. I have a fucking agenda. Everyone has a fucking agenda. I couldn't believe she'd said it so readily. These are the sorts of things we whisper in our sleep but never consciously, where people can hear.

*

I think about how many people I know who try to brush off the fact that their 'agenda' might be something that exists.

That it might be to tell a story that isn't just the same as everyone else's. The very idea of being accused of an agenda in itself: what a horrifying prospect. The idea that people might want to be heard! It was as if Karla, right there, had screamed at the top of her voice over almost everyone in the games industry. I have an agenda. I have a fucking agenda. I imagine her standing in front of an audience made up of everyone in attendance at the Game Developers Conference in San Francisco, and pointing at people: 'YOU have an agenda. And YOU have an agenda. And YOU have one too. I HAVE A FUCKING AGENDA.'

But Karla is quiet now, and is eating some chips. We make delirious ideas come to fruition: we should write a story about two women: one a fat, sexually vociferous woman, and one woman an acerbic androgynous wit, and together they will take over the narrative. Later I realise we have merely described a video game French and Saunders.

We went to the Animex Festival in Middlesbrough, where Karla had asked me to interview her in front of an audience about her work. I'd met her briefly for the first time at GDC a year ago, and this was only our second meeting. We get on well, because I think we both have a prickly uncertainty about our lives and a will to make jokes about the absurd. We joked about tampons, toilet rolls and pillows with skeletons in front of large audiences of students, and we showed trailers of Gun Home in between our talking about how Christmas Duck initially had too many polygons, as well as some useful stuff like how to use space and narrative.

Later in the bowels of a Mexican-themed bar over margaritas and bass-heavy music, I grill her on her beginnings. Karla started work in the games industry around 2000, working in animation for Turbine. Later she would go on to work on Bioshock 2: Minerva's Den at 2K Marin, doing narrative and 2D art. When Steve asked if she wanted to move to Portland, Oregon, to start The Fullbright Company with him, it seemed like a good time for a change, and so she moved into a house where the team all lived and worked.

'I wasn't in games originally, I was going to be in animation,' Karla says, the music vibrating over the banquette. 'I didn't know anything about games. I liked it, I still sort of like it, but it is a little more abstract.

'My dad used to make board games when I was a kid. Toy board games for me to mess with. And card games.' Karla says her dad recently made a political board game and sent it to the Fullbright house to test. 'We grew up playing Euro board games,' she says. 'There was a German game called World Trip which was about visiting a certain number of cities around the world map, and you had to stick push pins in the map where you'd been – it was actually kind of adorable. There was a game about ... I can't quite remember – it was a square board but the playing area was circular, and you would place cardboard trees in spots around. They had little clips for them so that they would stand up. And there was a wolf, and you had to stay out of his sight by staying behind the trees, and you had to try to get to a thing and pick up objects and stuff, and it was really cute. Maybe it was called "Pass auf, der Wolf!"? Which I remember being charming.'

I ask her if they have influenced the way she thinks about design: the mechanical parts of games, how play is mediated.

'Probably,' she says. 'It is really hard to know. I totally just took this stuff for granted. It never would have occurred to me to be "let's think about why we're playing board games in this family and how they work". It took me until much later to learn some design ideas, and learn to think about things productively.'

'How much animation do you still do?' I ask.

'I kind of burned out on it,' she says. 'This is extremely trivial, but when the book opens at the end of Gone Home, I did that – the pages sort of squoosh up. My background's in character animation. It's all balancing sides and secondary motions and stuff. All that kind of shit. I don't really do that much any more. I like to pay attention to it. I think, something isn't quite right about this, and I will ignore a medium until something interesting happens. That happens to me sometimes. I feel like finally people are getting the hang of stuff in Flash, even though it's been around forever. Maybe they're rediscovering it or something.

'I decided to do animation when I was in college. You get one year that's just foundation, all the basic shit that everybody has to go through,' Karla explains, before saying that was when she became interested in animation and chose it as her major. 'Because I went to art school I got zero basic education after that; it was all art-based. The foundation stuff was all figure drawing, sculpture, colour theory. I had to apply and send a portfolio. Going into my school, going into illustration, was sort of the default. Everyone went into that bin. [Animation] seemed to make sense at the time because it was just combining things ... I think I remember feeling like there is potential to have a job in animation rather than like sculpture or textiles, that stuff is pretty hard.

'I made all kinds of goofy stuff,' she goes on. 'At the beginning we did projects that were quite regimented, like rotoscoping, a cutout animation – say you have a little person and the torso's a piece and the upper legs are a piece and the bottom legs are a piece and the foot's a piece and you slowly move that across, and you slowly give it motion without having to redraw it. We did stop motion. I have little projects of these and they're all mouldering in 16mm in my parents' garage. My junior project in film was this really goofy thing where I got these two guys who worked with [me] at my work study job, and they were older than the students so I was totally proud of myself. I dressed them up in four different outfits and had this narrative which was that they were all after one thing, which was – like, which of course – because I was a derivative thinker and I still am, was a suitcase. However the one funny thing I did was that at the 'end when you open the suitcase, inside it was all the clothes they were wearing, so it was at least a little bit less dumb than it had to be. That film is called Octoglomerate.'

Karla tells me her influences at this time were Philip K Dick and Geof Darrow, hypermasculine hyperdetailed things. 'A lot of respecting only craft,' she says, sounding disappointed in herself. 'This was before Tarantino got really shitty. It's before I stopped liking him. I liked classic violent things. I was way better at dealing with that ... Nowadays I care more about interesting characters than I do about intricate plots and clever things. I loved the Coens when I was in college more than anything – *The Hudsucker Proxy* was my favourite because it's nothing but craft. It's solid. Everything is planned out perfectly and really cutely arranged. I thought that was like the best. I am pleased to say that I no longer think that way.'

I say her later growth of interest in character-led narrative must have been reflected in her work on Minerva's Den.

Art Karla made for Minerva's Den.

'Games are weird because they're sort of a world that you can work within – other things are sort of like that but ... how can I say it? Games are also more open-ended, and you have to worry about the world more by default in games. How things are put together. It's more about constructing a space in which things can happen. I understand editing and some amount of filmmaking, and it's really weird how people compare them all the time.'

I say I think games are much more about theatre than they are about film; the possibility space is much more explicit in both, they work live, they have an audience participating, there's a performative aspect. Steve Gaynor in particular gave a talk at GDC 2013's Level Design track about theatrical techniques used to direct player attention in Bioshock, for instance, things such as lighting, sound and movement as an indication of where the player should look and navigate. I think theatre in the round has much more to do with games than we've previously given credit for. Wrestling games, for example, seem like such a natural proposition. The player also often performs a role, as do NPCs.

'You really need to go to Sleep No More,' Karla says, with finality. 'When you are in the US. If I'm there, I will take you there.' As far as I can see, Sleep No More is a live theatre event that takes place in New York City, but I don't want to spoil it for myself too much. I am planning on travelling there in July. (I never do get to Sleep No More.)

Just before we got on the train back south from Animex, we got coffee, Karla bought Bakewell tarts (a British delicacy), and I told her I thought she was the closest likeness to a Daniel Clowes character I have ever met. She frowned, and then completely opened up. 'When I was a kid, when I was a teenager, I didn't realise that it was possible for me to identify with media. It was just like a foreign concept ... There wasn't a lot of stuff – stuff that influenced me – that I could actually identify with, and I just didn't like ... the concept didn't make any sense to me until I read *Ghost World* when I was in high school, and I was like, "Oh holy shit. This is actually for real, legit relatable." It was really strange.'

Our hotel room had some strange guests.

'Isn't it weird though,' I say, 'that a guy [Daniel Clowes] would be the person to write it?'

'Yes,' Karla says, sipping coffee, 'and another thing – *Heavenly Creatures*, which I saw in college, also about women, also written by a man – relatable. And that's the only thing I can think of offhand. And this was before I actually got to read good women writers – Alice Munro, Margaret Atwood and stuff. Because you know, I would read Philip K Dick and he couldn't write a female character to save his life – except *Man in the High Castle* which has the only good female character he's ever written. And so ... there was just like, nothing there. The idea of a role model was just kind of non-existent in the media that I tried to consume. I'm trying to think of what my conception of what I wanted to be was, and I think it was just kind of weird, androgynous invisible person, because I just wanted to not have the shitty lady trappings, and obviously it's not possible [for me] to just be a guy.'

I tell her I think a lot of my friends related to *Ghost World*. It's like the idea that girls could be sweary and be interesting and cool ...

'It's not quite that,' Karla says. 'It's more just like, we're shitty and we hate everything, this is somewhere I can actually see myself in the world, just kind of hate everything in the world, because that's how we used to operate back then. It was just kind of like, everything is basically dumb, but like, oh wait, that's me. It had never happened to me before. I was like, seventeen before that happened. Which is crazy.'

life. Essa has given up her rations to keep Boris alive, but in the end nothing can save him. Since the lining of the uterus is not needed for a pregnancy, it comes out through the vagina.

Essa vows to survive. She sets off to join the Polish resistance as a daring spy and saboteur. Another ovum starts to develop in one of the ovaries and the process begins again. It is incredible how the female body knows how to prepare for pregnancy!

Dee me!

I recall Sam's homework from Gone Home – the one about reproduction, where she winds a particularly earnest and somewhat imaginative narrative around the boring information about ovaries that she has to regurgitate. It ended in me laughing hard over how absurd she'd made the task. Karla's teenage 'I hate everything in the world' is deftly reflected in this one piece of homework. It's a masterpiece of satire, something that really tells you about Sam as a person, makes her much more relatable.

Karla asks me how I feel about characters I identified with. I tell her I probably didn't read *Ghost World* until two years ago when I moved in with comics artist Julia Scheele, and I feel similarly about it.

'Maybe this is more common than I think,' she says. She asks me about what I identified with growing up.

I say I always found solace in *Absolutely Fabulous*. For Eddy and Patsy, performing the role of 'femininity' wasn't so important as just being selfish; it was how male rock stars were supposed to behave, and Eddy and Patsy were doing it in their old age. Their outrageous sense of entitlement was something I so admired, because when you're a young woman you're persuaded you should sit down, shut up and look nice, but Eddy and Patsy took what they wanted loudly, and frankly didn't much give a shit whether their make-up looked shite after falling over themselves drunk to get it. They behaved more like the Rolling Stones than any of the so-called women role models I'd been presented with. And they were funnier than any women I'd ever seen on TV before. And they were a cast of all women.

'I've often found that British television is way better at depicting people who look like actual people,' Karla says. 'Like, often you can't be in media unless you're an attractive lady.'

Much of this conversation about *Absolutely Fabulous* has taken hold, because we buy a gratuitous bottle of Cava and two Creme Eggs to consume on the train back south.

As if to carry on the theme of women at a war council, we plan to meet Rhianna Pratchett, writer on Mirror's Edge, Tomb Raider and other impressive things, in the British Museum for afternoon tea that week.

Rhianna also introduced me to bubble tea,
which is weird and cool and rad.

Rhianna, over our dainty sandwiches and cute macarons, brings out the big guns. She has written some of the new Red Sonja comics, and the artist Naniiebim/ Louise Ho is illustrating. She tells me about Gerd, her warrior-turned-blacksmith.

Courtesy of Naniiebim/Louise Ho

Now this, I think, THIS is having a fucking agenda. We've got this. We've got this.

Embed with ...
Tim Rogers

An adventure in Oakland, California, living with game designer and prolific internet voice Tim Rogers.

Alleycat Blues

It's late and dark and Oakland, California. <u>Tim Rogers'</u> apartment glows with pastel light from the wall-size TV which shows his game Videoball in large font. Outside, the air is dry and breezy and lazy with the smell of freesias.

'Let's get In 'n' Out at the airport,' Starbaby hums, Jack Nicholson-like, his black mop looming in the pools cast from the blue lights that decorate Tim's apartment. Starbaby has a lot of teeth in his mouth; a personality like a Jack-in-the-box where the Jack is just knives. <u>Jazzpunk</u>'s Luis Hernandez stands nearby, his long dark hair and camera in his hand, agreeing because we're hungry and they've been playing Videoball all day with the sort of people everyone at the Game Developers' Conference last week would recognise. Tim's apartment is now quiet and a mess of pizza boxes, beer and energy drinks. I've been asleep all day, am drowsy. Vlambeer's Rami Ismail's bellowing laughter echoes through chambers of my skull.

Hali, Starbaby, Tim and me.
Photo: Luis Hernandez.

I look at Tim. He is wearing a purple and luminous green Michael Jordan sweater with long Michael Jordan shorts and socks to match. His hair is thick and dirty blond, his self-confessed best feature. His fingers are long and calloused with the nails cut deadly short so that they can bond with his cobalt blue Gibson, and his glasses are something out of a 1950s drama. Tim Rogers is a non-fiction anime character. He is a writer, co-creator of Insert Credit, the CEO of Action Button Entertainment, and he has worked in games, AAA and otherwise, all his adult life. He is thirty-four years old and is the internet's biggest rumour.

Tim says *heck yeah* and *we're gonna have a good time* and we crowd into Starbaby's repurposed cop car with no seatbelts and turn the music up as far as it will go.

Machine Guns in Tokyo

Tim Rogers loved music so much that after graduating in 2000 he moved to be near it in Tokyo. For the ten years he was there, complete strangers who read what he wrote about games and his life on the internet made pilgrimages to visit him. During that time Tim Rogers worked at Sony before winding up his time in Japan working as a designer for Grasshopper Manufacture under Goichi Suda. He left before he was credited on a game, and for a mysterious reason Tim's visa was not accepted on re-entry to the country in the end. But in that period Tim wrote reams and reams of words for a huge amount of outlets, for *Edge* magazine, GamesTM, Kotaku and many others. Not many people know very much about his work in big-budget game studios, because his writing about his life outside games and around the idiosyncrasies of games has always overshadowed practically everything else he has done. That's unfortunate to an extent, but it's real. People can tell when they're affected by Tim's writing, but they have no idea when they've played a game he's had a hand in.

One night Tim and I go for a midnight drive, nominally to a 24-hour Wal-Mart, but really it's just an excuse to get out. I ask Tim if now he'd play a Grasshopper Manufacture game that he'd worked on. He says he wouldn't, because it wasn't all his, and he thinks the development process was inherently flawed. Beside us the orange and white lights of Oakland pock the landscape by the highway, the red lights of the cars bleeding into reality, making it feel like we are underwater as we drive.

'I don't want to say I'm better at it than anyone else, or more experienced at it than anyone else, and I'm sure somebody'd hear me say this and call me some bad names in my email inbox,' Tim says, in a low tone of regret. 'I think I have a lot of experience thinking hypercritically about discomfort ... I feel like if I'm already sitting down to play a video game it's an uncomfortable process, it's not 100 per cent fluidly human to hold a controller and press a button to make something move on the TV screen ... A whole lot of weird, molecular-level strangeness, and I feel like you really can't trust a committee of people to work on that. Because what I think is uncool clashes with what somebody else thinks is not uncool. You end up making a whole lot of compromises. You do stuff by committee.

'It's not even committee,' he corrects himself. 'They would break out bullet points and say: "We're gonna talk about this.

We're gonna write a full-scale, full project-design document: so, there's a part about guns, because our game's got guns in it, and there's a part about the story, so let's see, why don't you write about the story, and you write about the guns, and, uh, you write about the jump button ..."

Zak McCune, Large Prime Numbers' drummer, and Tim.
Photo: Dan Tabar.

'And it's like, "here's the guns, sir," you know, like two days later,' Tim says, 'twenty-four guns. There's a pistol, heavy pistol, automatic pistol, machine gun, heavy machine gun, automatic machine gun, and then, y'know, flamethrower, silenced flamethrower – I'm actually listing actual guns that guy wrote down. He actually had "silenced flamethrower" on it … And I'd already written a game design document: there's four guns in this game and you can already use all of them and they all do these things that fit together.

'It would just be like, "Let's break up here, and you write about the heavy machine gun, and you write about the regular machine gun."'

Tim raises his voice. 'Why would you get different guys to write one-page game-feature proposal requests about two different types of machine gun? Wouldn't you want one guy designing all the machine guns? Just get a guy who likes and knows a whole lot about machine guns – there must be somebody around there.

'It's just kind of filthy with indecision, all the games I've worked on previously,' Tim concludes. 'My name's not on any of 'em. I got an email last week from a guy: "I just beat No More Heroes 2, and your name wasn't in the credits" – it's like, yeah, I know. Yeah, so I don't like those games. I think they're kind of tacky and sloppy … Lacking in a unity of vision.'

Suda once requested that Tim write a 'gigolo system' for a game because EA had requested 'original features', which Tim did write up. This system is the one that was eventually implemented in Killer Is Dead and is still documented in a vintage Gdoc Tim showed me. Tim wasn't credited for that either, in the tradition of AAA studios only crediting those employees who were there when the game was shipped. But it's not something I'd want my name on either, I guess.

Strangers in Tokyo

Me, Tim and Tim's long-time friend Lily Wang.
Photo: Luis Hernandez.

After a week I'm about ninety per cent sure not even Tim really knows why his writing has had this attracting effect on people over the years. I am still floundering around in the ten per cent. I suspect it's the scimitar-sharp honesty, slow-poison sentences, acute intelligence, an intense enjoyment of language, and a large dose of humour and generosity, but no one can really be sure. I once commented in the car park at the Berkeley Bowl where Tim buys salsa that I think we both make money from being honest on the internet. He said, 'I'm honest about the things that the internet doesn't like.'

People made pilgrimages to see him is what I wrote down, a few paragraphs up.

This idea seems unreal to me, because all in all Tim is just a person, a person that outside video games probably not that many people know. He's a person I know and like – an acquaintance I'd hang out with if I were in town and I had a few hours to kill. But that strangers came to see him in Tokyo like they did and, to a certain extent, still do in his new place in Oakland, just because of their infatuation with his writing: that's unreal, even though I was one of the people who made the 'pilgrimage' when I moved to Japan in 2008, even though I sought him out in Tokyo, even though at one point I thought he was fictional and had to shake his hand to see if he was real, even though every half-joke he makes is sort of a painful truth, even though young dumb Cara sat over cold soba and enthused about *Doctor Who* with him and wondered why she cared because everyone did that. Everyone back then did that.

Let's Kick Shell

None of the essays Tim has ever written specifically about games have been his best prose works, but people only know of him because of those things. They know him from Kotaku, from his troll-wrangling, from his outrageous games commercials, from his dissections of missed games. But what's refreshing about Tim as a game designer is that there's a healthy vein running through all the games and prototypes he makes that pulsates directly from the heart of his games analysis. You don't have to interview him in a thirty-minute press junket to understand what Tim likes about games. You can just read from his own intensely detailed hand the individual moments of others' work he found fascinating, satisfying or rewarding. There's a pattern in the sort of things Tim likes to lyricise about. Take his Godhand review (which he also played the backing track for).

Godhand is the catharsis of using a jackhammer to cut your birthday cake.

Almost all of the analogies he uses to describe Godhand are to do with objects of weight and momentum, things designed to elicit sensation, feedback, collision. Tim also once wrote an essay about 'sticky friction' ('Sticktion') that I have used as an all-purpose tool of my games criticism trade ever since: the idea that games have a unique ability to feed back certain types of 'friction' that are rewarding to the player. 'It was all about the inertia, the acceleration, the to-a-halt-screeching when you change direction,' Tim said of Super Mario Brothers. 'You can feel the weight of the character. People never put these feelings into words when talking about games, though they really, really are everything.'

Much of our time was spent making late-night trips to Target and finding the most absurd items to Instagram, which is more fun than you might think.

'I sort of feel bad about writing that,' Tim says to me on our midnight trip to the Wal-Mart that would prove to be closed. 'I could have just been working on games and could have kept that all to myself. Even at GDC this year I got a bunch of people coming up to me and these people are making these really fantastic-looking games and they're like, "Yeah, man, we read your Sticky Friction thing, man, we talk about it all the time." It's like, man, what the heck, y'know?

'That was kind of a light analysis of some aspects of design: it's the comfort thing. Textiles, past a certain point. Cos you're just talking about the feel of it ... I was trying to have fun writing that. "I'll put this on Kotaku." And then I get all these really serious cool people coming up to me and being like, "Oh yeah, I read that and it changed the way I think about this thing".'

Tim frowns. 'Man, did I just give a bunch of incredibly talented people really good advice that they can use to be more successful in the field that I am attempting to become successful in?'

Us in the cop car. We were pulled over by the actual cops at Oakland airport for driving aimlessly in a cop car with no licence plates.
Photo: Luis Hernandez.

Tim goes on to tell me that students attending Indiecade this year told him his writing on Super Mario Brothers 3 is being taught in classes at NYU. And there's no doubt in my mind that his analysis of that game is sharp – he's written three essays on it. Zero in on where the friction is in a game, and how it's rewarding, and you've got a good piece of games criticism. Equally, find the games that have the most 'Sticktion' and chances are they will be the most rewarding in terms of base 'enjoyment', if that's what you look for in your games. Both Ziggurat and Videoball make heavy use of 'Sticktion' and this isn't a coincidence. Sticktion's sort of what Tim lives on, down to the choice of keyboard he types on at his computer, the socks he buys, the games he wants to make.

The Technodrome

I've played Tim's upcoming game Videoball, something he's making with the talented Double Fine programmer Ben Burbank. Minimalist interface, one button and analogue stick input, one screen competitive play: a cross between Hokra and Asteroids. There's huge tactical depth in this game to the extent that on release it could become an instant and incredibly popular e-sport. It's got evolving metagame, and it has local and online modes. It's easy to pick up, very easy to understand, but takes a long time to master the layers of the game. Playing Videoball feels closer to the actual feel of soccer than soccer simulations like Fifa. There's a slide and grind to the game that speaks to the Sticky Friction Tim wrote about. You press and hold A to charge a shot: it has three power levels, the highest being an across-the-screen punt that's got a satisfying weight to it. The game manufactures loud screams and smack-talk and the sort of rage that Mario Party induces. It makes Vlambeer's Rami Ismail yell at the top of his voice. It fills Tim's apartment with people. It makes people who think they don't understand games feel like they understand games. It's good. It's really good.

Make a Video Game, Write a Book

McCune and Tim. Photo: Dan Tabar.

Do you think your writing about games influences the way you think about making games? I ask Tim. I'm thinking of Jim Rossignol, Tom Francis – all the people successfully making small-budget games who used to be critics for a living.

'I always wanted to make a video game and I always wanted to write a book,' Tim says. 'I decided to just start taking notes when I was playing video games. I don't know why it started for the purpose of "taking notes": I had no concept of putting a review up on the internet. I was just taking note of stuff I noticed and somehow I was wording them as sentences. Just having fun pairing words together. I've always had fun pairing words. I enjoy writing sentences, not necessarily paragraphs.

'Early on it was on paper. There was a website I liked, the Gaming Intelligence Agency, the GIA. They were all talking about "video game journalism sucks" in 1996/97... I read those websites for my video game news and I thought it's cool how those people think about video games. There was a letters column on that website and I loved writing the letters column... The letters column was cool because it was run by the staff of the website, just college students like me, but they had a website, and the website had a cool beige background which was cool because websites back then had all-white backgrounds ... You know, they dressed your letter up and made it look nice.'

Tim's style wasn't so much influenced by the GIA, but he said the GIA indicated that this kind of writing on the internet was possible. And it helped him form his taste.

'I wanted to get on the forum and I wanted to say some stuff and have these conversations with people,' he says. 'Mostly it was kind of a subconscious process of figuring out what I don't like. Any creative process, you'll have decisions you're going back and forth on, and you have to decide: what don't I like, am I trying to extract what I don't like, or am I trying to focus on what I do like? I end up going back and forth on that a lot, and I sort of figure out what sort of game I want ... It sounds really jerky, but I couldn't find a game that directly perfectly appealed to what I wanted. Not saying that what I wanted was the universal best game, like some Da Vinci Code, some universal code of games ...'

I mention that Toni Morrison stated she wrote the book she wanted to read, and that this perhaps is the approach that many people might have to their games: making the game that's missing from the shelf. Tim says he likes Toni Morrison. Then he tells me apparently Mel Gibson only watches his own films, and then enquires as to whether Toni Morrison only reads her own books. I don't actually know, I say. I've never heard a sentence containing the words 'Toni Morrison' and 'Mel Gibson' before.

Carebears

Tim owns a lot of Carebears. Carebears: the stuffed toys. He just likes them. He likes the look of them. It's not an affectation, or if it is, he insists it isn't. What I do know is that his parents are scared that he is gay, and so is the internet. His offbeat tastes are somehow destabilising to internet masculinity, and the homophobia directed towards Tim, who as far as I know has never dated men, is sort of incredible.

Death threats and insults to his inbox after articles are common (he tells me that after writing about Final Fantasy XIII for Kotaku someone got his address and emailed him to tell him he was coming to slit his throat). There's a real pulsating hatred out there directed towards Tim, and he navigates it sort of cheerfully, telling me that the blog that his best prose has always appeared on, Large Prime Numbers, is consistently hacked every single time he puts up a new article there, and so he doesn't put anything there any more. This also appears to have elicited even more angry emails demanding to know why Tim isn't writing there any more.

The American Dream

In 'n' Out, Oakland. Photo: Luis Hernandez.

It's just after 1 a.m. We pull into In 'n' Out by Oakland airport, Starbaby's at the wheel, his Japanese James Dean jaw casting a shadow in the bleaching fluorescence of the fast food joint. 'Whaddaya want?' he says. Tim is miming guitar riffs in the back of Starbaby's cop car to 'Big Apple 3 a.m.'. In the front passenger seat Luis is grinning.

Starbaby is a nickname given to him by Tim. Starbaby is someone who visited Tim in Tokyo after reading Tim's work. This is often the answer to the question of how Tim knows anyone. Starbaby tells me later that he's been reading Tim Rogers' work since he was sixteen years old. Starbaby is a year younger than me, at twenty-seven, but has known Tim for most of his life, first by internet and then in Tokyo, and then in Oakland. Tim and Starbaby have a kind of symbiotic relationship now, to the extent that Tim says he 'insinuated' Starbaby into working a job at his favourite doughnut place, Pepples in Oakland, just so that he could get free doughnuts.

We park and open the doors of the car so the music vibrates out onto the tarmac, and we eat fries and burgers and drink shakes by the lit black sky, starched and drawn by the airport nearby. The music is so loud we shout at each other.

'THIS IS THE AMERICAN DREAM,' Luis Hernandez yells at me, a mouth full of animal fries and ears full of Turtles In Time. Luis is Canadian. He is being ironic. But both he and I know it has a weird resonance.

Later Luis tells us he likes Oakland better than San Francisco. 'San Francisco is fake, like GTA. The pedestrians seem like they have predestined pathways,' he says. 'Oakland's more real.'

'Like *Wayne's World*,' I say, as a joke, because we're all in a car, and then realise that I sort of mean it. The fictional Aurora, Illinois, seems like a place that's more real than San Francisco, a land of startups and mirror shades.

Starbaby's cop car suspension cushions the twist up and up and up the mountain, and the burger in my stomach mashes itself against my insides.

Tim and I are thrown around in the back with no seatbelts on like bottletops in the bowels of a corkscrewing ship, Tim holding on to the umbilical cord of the wire that sends music from his iPhone to the car's sound system. He flaps it around. 'This is how I like to think about games,' he says, indicating the new track he is feeding the speakers, waggling the line, the dash responding to his touch.

Starbaby smacks the wheel. 'YOU SHOULD WRITE THAT DOWN!' he yells at me and I laugh.

All of a sudden Oakland is a constellation below us.

Photo: Luis Hernandez.

We slide to a stop on a patch of dirt by the road. There are other cars around us with people in them in the murk, but we ignore them, wary of the intrusion. There's a huge tree trunk lodged in the side of the mountain carved into a seat, and Starbaby gets on top of it to look at the lights, and says, 'I once came up here on Valentine's Day and I saw a guy stand on top here, crush a can in his hands and throw it away, and say, "I'm so happy I'm not in jail any more".'

Tim accuses him of making it up.

'It's the truth,' Starbaby says.

Part of me is certain that they have taken me here because they think when I tell this story it will sound like I made it up. Or perhaps they knew it was always going to be written down, and wanted to make it look like they live in some kind of Diablo Cody script. But I've been here a week, and this doesn't seem unusual for them at all.

Dinosaur Sweater

It seems stupid to regard Tim as magnetic or influential or important, but the worst thing about all these thoughts is that after six years of knowing of him, about him, and finally living with him, it scares me to think that he might be all of these things to a generation of digital adherents on the internet, and he's just a human fucking being. Someone who will be dead one day. Someone who just writes on the internet and makes games for a living. It's extraordinary that these are all thoughts I think about Tim when he's just some jerk who is right now as I speak ordering trashy pizza from Little Caesar's and said his ideal woman is 'Dora the Explorer eleven years later' and keeps referring to me facetiously as 'world-famous games journalist Cara Ellison' because of my Twitter followers and has a fridge full of almond butter and thinks it's okay to make fun of how shit I am at playing the game that he is currently developing that hasn't been released yet. He'd want me to resent him, I think. I think I do.

Probably some people who visited Tim in Tokyo thought, like George Clooney's bed partners, that they were the *only one*, but the reality is that whole forums of people visited Tim during that ten-year period, some of them now prominent digital wordstitchers, artists, loaded Silicon Valley denizens. More and more of them reveal themselves to me as time goes on, though very few people would be able to say from their stay that they got to know him. This is because Tim's entire persona is constructed of streams and streams of words, puns, jokes that are directed at you, launched into you, things that he lays on you. Words are a thick paste that Tim paints over everyone he comes across, and it's equal parts thrilling and exhausting and occasionally feels like an outlandish contraceptive so that you can't really get much of him at all.

Tim is a psychedelic knitted dinosaur sweater where the wool is words. He is constructed of words. This probably doesn't surprise you if you've ever read his work, which drives Kotaku commenters mad with rage at the sheer word count. Tim gets up and writes every day into his hard drive, and publishes less and less of it these days. It's as if, if he stops producing words he's afraid that he might not exist any more. (This is a fear that many writers have, in their hearts, I think.) But for Tim, it probably comes from being mute between the ages of eleven to seventeen, all the way through puberty. He's making up for lost time, maybe. He's talking because he found his voice and he has it on a leash now. He's tied it up in a basement. Tim's voice is his now and it's so sharp and omnipresent and alive and, in the dark moments, upset, it could slice steel into fine slivers.

Under Streets

It's dark in the apartment. The hum of the bathroom fan undulates through the wall. I say to Tim that I miss the green tea Kit Kats that Family Marts in Japan used to stock.

He tells me a story in a low quiet voice.

Not long ago he went back to Japan, years after he was denied entry into the country, the country he lived in for ten years. He stayed in a hotel in Tokyo near his old commute to the Sony office, and he bought a Snickers and a Kit Kat and a Crunky, and he ate them in bed, just like he used to in Japan before he was denied a visa. He lay in the hotel bed and thought about the Sony office being just down the street. Just down the street from the hotel. And yet, he would never go back in that building.

I try to find something to say, but there is nothing in my mouth and I can feel a horrible pain in my chest, a membrane breaking in my throat. I think I left something of myself in Japan too, but it's not as much of me as it is for Tim. I feel like Tim left a limb there. I feel like Tim left a liver. Or a kidney. A heart. Parts of him are chained up raw under Tokyo's streets and people walk over them every day.

There are very few things in Tim's Oakland apartment that are from Japan, though he lived there for ten years. The only things are his very small collection of Japanese video games, and a picture of him and the Green-Haired Girl.

When there's nothing left to say I have a sudden terrifying thought: what on earth am I going to write about him that Tim couldn't write down himself? The terror of having another person, also a writer, a good writer, read my writing about him, is suffocating. But apparently I've said it out loud.

'You'll think of something,' Tim says, senpai-like.

There are many ways in which Tim Rogers is interesting. I haven't been able to write all of them down. I think Tim will write them down for me.

Pepples Donut Farm – Hali, Tim, Starbaby and me at breakfast.
Photo: Luis Hernandez.

Things Tim says often:

'The best thing about parking at the STOP sign is, when you get in your car, you can just go.' (He said this multiple times. Every time we got in the car, actually.)

'Never party on someone else's terms.'

Embed with ...
Katharine Neil and
Harvey Smith

I lurk on the edges of Paris, not quite an inhabitant, not quite an outsider. Alexandre Lejeune, a friend of a friend, has just left me, and it's raining over the neon of the Chinese and Vietnamese restaurants. Rumour has it the best bars are at the Bastille, but I choose Place d'Italie and Saint-Denis to lurk. I live for the moments in between, where Cat Power sings to me in silvered tones about rambling and being a woman, just so I can be alone and think about the conversations.

I am full to burst of conversation. I am full to burst of stories, stories about games culture and how to negotiate a bank balance stuck on nothing. Of a full four weeks to the brim on stories of young travel and accidental marriage and anarchy and how the French love and hate.

Rewind.

I woke on top of a chiptune artist that morning with a letter for the US embassy and a dreadful hangover. I took two buses taking two hours in the London tube strike while trying to avoid throwing up on small children; when I explained to the US embassy that I write about games for a living the woman laughed and said, 'Well, somebody has to' and they stamped ISSUE, hell, yes, and I took a train to Middlesbrough and interviewed Karla Zimonja tired in bars, threw all my belongings out of my Brighton house and packed two bags from the debris, flew them to California and sat in cars and over late-night doughnuts with Tim Rogers for weeks, flew to AMAZE Berlin and woke up at 4 a.m. to Chipzel sweating post-gig in my hotel room, a packet of crisps in her hand, fell back asleep and I was holding a glass of Merlot in Rue du Faubourg, Paris, next to a couple trying to eyefuck each other into orgasm. There is no chiptune artist here, either naked or eating crisps. I look, dazed, at the wine in my hand.

Ah, Paris. Are you there, Paris? I try to slide my foot near it under the table. Paris is that tall man with the five o'clock shadow who believes in the 'chase'. Paris is a mind older than Oakland, much craftier than London.

A Temple for all our Gods

The story begins in a place called Bouillon Chartier. I sit opposite New Zealand-born game developer Katharine Neil. We've ordered champignons and the cheapest wine on the menu, and I am trying to defend US-born Deus Ex designer Harvey Smith. Both Katharine and Harvey live here in France. They are both on The List.

'People should know who Harvey is,' Katharine says, horrified, surrounded by enclaves of brass and wood, the roof high and old.

'There's a temple for all of our gods, big and small, past and present,' I say, the cut of steak knives through bloody meat around us. 'And pretty much everyone goes there for inspiration ... But the statues were never inscribed in the first place, unless you're Cliff Bleszinski, maybe Warren Spector. That's just how it is.' There shouldn't be a canon, but there always ends up being one, and it's never enough. And the people who decide it are always the ones with the money.

Katharine has been telling me she is unsurprised to hear that no one has heard of her, but she is appalled that anyone who makes games would ask who Dishonored's Harvey Smith is. Yet Katharine Neil is the never-heard-of game developer that everyone should know about. I shift uncomfortably every time Katharine self-denigrates, which is often.

Hidden by the Square Jaw of Kip Neil

Katharine Neil has been developing games since 1998. A professional game designer, sound designer and programmer: a triple threat if you will. She worked on a string of AAA titles in Australia for places like Atari and Infogrames, and switched in and out of various roles in development. Alongside her work in the commercial industry, she created game-based artwork and fostered game development within the Australian arts community: Katharine co-founded Free Play in 2004 with Marcus Westbury, Australia's now annual independent game developers conference. She's now in Paris completing her PhD in Tools for Game Design at Conservatoire national des arts et métiers and Flinders University in South Australia, and has worked with Lady Shotgun Games on Buddha Finger as well as producing her own projects.

She's also the most politically opinionated developer I've ever met.

In 2003 Katharine, veteran current affairs journalist Kate Wild, veteran designer Ian Malcolm, and a team of extremely talented game developers risked their jobs and future careers to make the political sucker-punch game Escape From

Woomera. Katharine was the creative director. The Half-life mod prototype explored the real-life injustices of asylum seekers who were imprisoned in the Woomera Detention Centre in Australia in direct defiance of UN stipulations. It provides the player with a way to experience the difficult situations and understand the decisions of someone up against the bureaucracy and injustice of the state. The aim is to get out of the detention centre, something only a few asylum seekers had done at the time. Asylum seekers were asked to contribute their stories and they were interpreted into the game design as accurately as possible. You can play the prototype through as several different asylum seekers, who each reveal different stories and ways to escape.

Escape From Woomera.

The Australian Council for the Arts awarded $25,000 to the team to have Escape From Woomera developed. This was not a popular decision with the Australian Minister of Immigration Phillip Ruddock, or the head of the Refugee Council of Australia, Margaret Piper. Ruddock thought the game would make Australia look bad (as opposed to the real policies the game portrayed in detail), and Piper thought that because it was a video game it would 'trivialise' the issue – a popular opinion amongst the conservative left. The team was called on by Channel Nine, the *Today Show*, ABC Radio, *The Age* and several other media outlets to justify themselves. The New York Times wrote a feature on games that it said depicted a new 'grim reality'. It was the largest ideological fistfight a game had ever instigated: bare knuckle with a government, using its own funding. It told the Australian government in no uncertain terms that if games aren't art they certainly mean something.

Years later Daniel Golding at ABC would write an excellent retrospective on the controversy. Woomera Detention Centre has now been shut down, but other detention centres have been consolidated in its wake. The game's website has been placed in an Australian national internet archive called Pandora, a place I like to imagine is the online version of the warehouse from *Raiders of the Lost Ark*.

'The Minister for Culture ordered an inquiry into how the project could be funded,' Katharine says to me while she cooks in her tiny Saint-Denis kitchen. 'The Minister for Immigration said what we were doing was illegal, because we were encouraging refugees to break the law.'

What good's an honest soldier if he can be ordered to behave like a terrorist? – Deus Ex

The media frenzy began when Katharine answered questions on the game anonymously for the *Sydney Morning Herald*. She was working for Atari at the time, and she remained anonymous throughout Woomera's development for fear of losing her job. She suspected she would be fired if she went public because a year earlier she'd written a political article entitled 'Fight to the death: military versus the modder' criticising the first person shooter America's Army, and her boss brought her into his office and warned her that she shouldn't be writing political screeds. When Katharine co-founded Freeplay in 2004, she sat in the audience of her own talk on Escape From Woomera and answered questions on her laptop via text-to-speech to retain her anonymity, like something from a spy film.

'I regret not having the balls to go, oh fuck it, if I get the sack then, whatever,' Katharine says now. 'I'd have had more of a profile.' She considers that now perhaps her authority and credibility to change things would be greater.

Few people in games have heard of Katharine. She was afraid that if people knew her name, she would lose her livelihood. Until recently Katharine was undercover <u>on Twitter</u> as hot Aussie bloke 'Kip Neil', her disguise a picture of the most square-jawed man she could find for an avatar (she tells me this was part of an experiment to see if people really do listen more to men). (When she first started to talk to me on Twitter under this guise I was delighted, so perhaps it works.)

Escape From Woomera was only a prototype mod, but its legacy managed to create a conversation that forced people to consider games as a cultural force for deeper thought. 'That was the main conversation people were having in the comment threads,' Katharine says when I ask her if it changed people's perception of games. 'The idea that games might not just be commercial! That they might be culturally relevant. People went from "urgh, you're a game developer" to changing their minds. The idea that you could even fucking string a sentence together, that you could have serious ideas and don't want to corrupt the children ...'

The Australian public got behind the idea, even if the government didn't. People started to ask each other if games were art, even if they didn't quite believe it. A few key people in the establishment stood up for the project. But some people with funding in the cultural establishment tried, in the beginning, to prevent Katharine's team from making Escape From Woomera.

Katharine shakes her head. '"You can't make entertainment out of serious issues," they said. Charlie Chaplin made *The Great Dictator*! The number of people who told me beforehand – *you can't do this, you can't do this, you can't do this. Maybe you could do this ten years from now. Maybe you could do it if it's not a game.*

'One woman said, "We don't fund mass market projects." I said, "Well, it's an art project." "But it's a game." "It's political. It's art. It's got political content." "We're a bi-partisan organisation."

'I was thinking, you work for an arts organisation, Jesus fucking Christ,' she continues. 'The amount of people who said, "You can't do it. You won't be able to do it. You should just give up."'

But she did do it. She did it anyway.

To Lyon

Harvey by Lyon graffiti

This isn't a training exercise, JC. Your targets will be human beings. – Deus Ex

'I'm glad you're writing about Katharine,' <u>Harvey Smith</u> would say to me in his Lyon apartment. 'I've known Katharine Neil since something like 2001, and I feel like everyone in video games should know who she is. Around that time I bumbled into Escape From Woomera, and Beyond Manzanar. And people like Katharine were taking things like the Doom engine and making more meaningful installation-type work with those things. Those were proto-art games, proto-indie games. Leah and I have visited her a couple of times since we moved here. I love our conversations.'

Harvey Smith was a keynote speaker/guest speaker on a panel about politics in games at Freeplay, when Katharine organised it in 2004. 'Katharine taught me the term "the dog's breakfast", talking about politics in the early 2000s, and I will always be grateful,' he says.

'It was good for me to meet Harvey,' Katharine would tell me later. 'I'd never met such a non-blokey games designer before. I was like, wow, in America they have games designers who are vegetarians, and who talk about feelings.'

Now that I have spent a good amount of time living with Harvey and Katherine it's obvious that they like each other and admire each other. They are both used to scraping by on nothing, both used to using the wiles they have to claw their way into life. 'I got married once,' Katharine once dropped in over lunch, 'for the bigger student allowance ... I should probably get divorced.'

Harvey and Katharine are both chameleons, adjusting to their environment and gathering what they can to make the things they need to make. They have lived in various different countries; different world governments have shaped their thoughts wherever they went. It's made them care about others deeply. There's a greatly empathetic working-class politic that weaves bright through both Katharine and Harvey's wakes.

Bravery is not a function of firepower. – Deus Ex

In 2006 Harvey won the GDC Game Design Challenge against other notables, Epic's Cliff Bleszinski and Katamari Damacy's Keita Takahashi, for Peace Bomb. It was a sneaknet-based grassroots organising game arbitrated (hypothetically) through handheld consoles. But this wasn't a one-off. Harvey's game design history is peppered with a particular cynicism of government control (Deus Ex), a deep and personal expression of the rich–poor divide (Dishonored), and an expression of anxiety over violence as a solution to anything runs deep through both. This latter point in particular is still unusual in big-budget video games, even today. Harvey displays a constant engagement through his work and personal life with political issues. Currently Harvey resides at Arkane, where he enjoys a close creative partnership with Raphael Colantonio, whom he often speaks warmly of.

'Me and Raph were always talking about the crushed per cent of the population, scrabbling for their lives,' Harvey says of Dishonored's development. 'I think all of that circles around. It influences you in some way.'

Harvey Smith is one of our very best in the murky echelons of publisher-funded large-scale works. His considerable life experience before video games is woven into the fabric of the games he makes. To hear Harvey speak about the state of US politics is to understand a great deal about how frustrated he is with the way things are, but also to understand exactly why, though he grew up immersed in conservative ideologies, he slowly came to have a progressive outlook on life. Throughout my stay Harvey and I often talk about feminism and how games can be made to represent women better.

It's apparent that Harvey has had a pretty hard life. He was born on the Gulf Coast to a fifteen-year-old mother who died of a drug problem when Harvey was six. He moved in with his father, a welder, who was abusive toward Harvey and eventually took his own life. Harvey couldn't afford to go to college, and so joined the Air Force and was posted to Germany, where he found solace in the books his literature professor proscribed – 'Nabokov, Alice Walker'. It made him into a writer. After his first marriage ended, he met Leah, someone who aside from being his intellectual equal, seems to challenge him and support him, and is an important pillar of the Austin games community in her own right. They are now married and live together in Lyon, France.

Door in Lyon.

But Harvey is quick to point out that he only began to get things together in his life when he turned thirty – after seven years of therapy to repair the damage that his early life caused him. He talks about how blessed he feels now, to do things such as go to London and walk around grand old buildings in his research for Dishonored. 'I appreciate that so much,' he says. 'I don't think most people in games realise, I don't think even most games journalists realise, relative to people on the planet ... If you add up the seven billion people on the planet, and you build a pyramid, the conceptual base being the bulk of the people and the conditions that they live in to this pinnacle where like Gwyneth Paltrow lives ... I think most people would be shocked to see where they are on that. Many of us are just incredibly lucky. Incredibly privileged.'

I ask Harvey candidly why he hasn't 'gone indie' yet. His taste in games more often corresponds with small-budget games than AAA. 'A lot of the games I really love right now are indie games,' he says, while I fiddle with Steam. 'Of the indie games I encounter I probably love about fifteen per cent of them. Of the triple A games I encounter I probably like two per cent of them or something. There are different constraints for both as a developer, whether you're a triple A path or an indie path. But when a game works for me it doesn't matter to me, whether it's Red Dead Redemption or Sir, You Are Being Hunted, there's something I'm chasing. Last year my favourite games were Gone Home and Papers, Please, but I also played State of Decay.'

Describing his past to me, Harvey says that an important consideration is how your background contextualises your feelings about what you do for a living. He explains that if you grew up in a very privileged family where everyone has very high expectations of you, you might never be satisfied with any one place in the world. But come from the Gulf Coast and have a life like his, and you might consider yourself very lucky to be where you are, working with good people under good conditions.

Our conversation turns to funding, one of the reasons Harvey says he is wary of going independent.

'A really complicated piece of it is: how do you fund it?' he says. 'It's really easy to say, oh just do it ... But everyone's circumstances are different. I have younger friends now – I'm not exaggerating – who have a hundred thousand dollars of student loan debt. Conversely I know people who live on trust funds. I also know people who live on a couch and just starved for three years to make it work. I know people who very cleverly worked in AAA for a while, paid off their house, got renters for their house and used that as a supplementary income.'

The US in particular can be a risky place to 'go indie' when important support such as healthcare is provided through companies instead of taxes.

'The US makes it very easy to start businesses if you already have access to funds and all,' Harvey says. 'If you do really well, you keep all of the money. But on the other hand the safety net and the things that people in the US see as a fundamental right are limited. It can be frustrating. I look at this like a game designer. If you looked at all the levers that you have in terms of a GDP, you could tweak it so that off the very high end you take some money and put it on the low end, so that everybody has a base subsistence. If you get sick you're taken care of, and if you're elderly you're taken care of, or you have a year of maternity leave. Things like that stabilise a society. It enables people to take more risks. I'm living in France right now, and I'm working with a guy who took a few years off to be an actor and eventually he ended up in video games. Now he draws from both of those fields.'

'Pas de culture sans droit sociaux'

It's odd that I should be here in France to see these two people, because before I arrived I had no idea how much their ideologies complement each other. One would almost think that at France's heart it encourages political engagement, one would almost think that its culture and indulging of the arts and its outlook on the world and endorsement of people's entitlement – nay, right – to joy would encourage a certain type of person to move from the country of their birth to sit and talk with like minds.

'No culture without social rights'

63

When I first got to Katharine's flat in Saint-Denis, her flatmate Marion wasn't around. Marion was out at a demonstration with a friend. France's *intermittents* were demonstrating in a squat.

Intermittents are those who get a certain amount of unemployment 'insurance' from the French government in return for working in certain arts, like theatre or dance, sometimes digital installations. France is currently reforming this legislation. The reform is going to reduce the money they are given. Marion's friend is an actor.

There is a sense in France that everyone has a right to joy, and that art helps spread this joy. Joy is government supported. At a tulip festival in Saint-Denis, for example, there was a forest set up like a little fair with wooden analogue games for children to play, and they are rewarded with small slide shows or music for 'winning' – putting the ball in the hole, or for negotiating a maze.

There was an elaborate carousel set up that was exquisitely made – all moving parts and hinges on a wooden owl's wings that a young girl could flap. France thinks that everyone has the right to play.

Wooden merry-go-round at a local Saint-Denis fair

Unfortunately, this does not entirely extend to video games yet, although la Gaîté lyrique, a digital arts and modern music centre in Paris, does a little to display games' promise.

Human beings may not be perfect, but a computer program

with language synthesis is hardly the answer to the world's problems. – Deus Ex

Katharine Neil has moved away from attempting to make overtly political games and into her own projects, such as the narrative-led <u>Alone In The Park</u> and several other prototypes for mobile and PC. This is partly because she felt burned by her earlier efforts, but also because the direction the 'social impact' game industry is taking is not to her liking. In the past Katharine has been a <u>critic</u> of Games For Change, beginning with when a game awarded a prize by Games For Change, <u>Urgent Evoke</u>, was funded and co-designed by the World Bank. At one point in her life, Katharine was teargassed by the World Bank. 'Paolo [Pedercini] said this <u>a few days ago in his talk</u>,' she says. 'He said these big NGOs, these aren't my politics. I feel the same.'

Why make games, then? Are games still an extension of the political self, even if you do not explicitly set out to send a political message? The old saying that the personal is political, is worn, but it's still true that unless games are very personal or focus on one particular life outlook, they lack a narrative punch. And when they do have narrative punch it often has political implications. Papers, Please, and Gone Home, two of Harvey's favourite games, are games that show very clearly that the personal is politically provocative. Papers, Please shows the ramifications of one border control person's decisions on whole nations and families, while Gone Home explicitly sets out to tell the story of a young queer girl, a narrative long neglected by games.

Harvey's games clearly show that, narratively, ordinary people and their decisions matter to him, and throughout the dialogue and systems in both Deus Ex and Dishonored a struggle is shown: that of people struggling to get by and a constant awareness of how human bonds may influence outcomes. In the very beginning of Deus Ex, the player is urged by a character to consider NPCs as 'human beings' rather than terrorists, and how much you adhere to this has ramifications throughout all the game's systems. Deus Ex is a prime example of using systems, the CCTV systems, or AI systems, in order to have a different outcome, just as he talked about in his analysis of the US wealth imbalance. He is in it for the struggle. For the switch flipping. For how those little situations can become meaningful, larger than themselves.

But games can also bring a sense of fulfilment to the player from negotiating systems in a way that is satisfying, even thrilling, in a way that sometimes life is not.

'[Games can be] this series of desperate improvisational actions where you have to get creative and do something under duress that makes your heart race, raises goosebumps,' he says. 'State Of Decay recently gave me that from one of their most trivial missions, just because of the systems involved. It was me interacting with systems in a very dramatic way. The game gave me just enough tools to solve the problem in a creative way. It was incredibly difficult. And it was like when I played Farcry 2. It was that experience. But only rarely do games give me that big, first-person, systems-driven experience in a coherent, convincing world, with a good sense of movement and "sticky friction"... We specifically made Dishonored, from a place of passion, to do all of that.'

But even though Katharine stopped making explicitly political games, they are still political to her. The act of creation is political to her.

'Games are the artform of our time,' she tells me, late at night. 'I wanted to be a concert pianist when I was young, but in terms of class and history ... what would I be giving to anyone? It's what people are doing in the world now. They're playing games.

'I do love opera, especially seventeenth-century French

opera, and I did want to become an opera singer, and I learned baroque opera singing. However, your audience ... I just want to be engaged with contemporary culture. And I want to make culture.'

'It's a class thing as well for me,' she elaborates. 'Games, arcades and stuff that I remember from growing up in the eighties – playing a game while waiting for your fish and chips. It was a real working-class art.

'Games are the underdog artform. Culturally, I feel comfortable there.'

Despite pleas from certain [Freeplay] speakers that the role of independent game development is to fill the niches that are not profitable for the large publishers, there seems to be a long way to go before the notion of independent game development being able to co-exist alongside commercial games development is an acceptable mantra. – PC Powerplay, *issue 102, 2004*

Embed with ...
Liz Ryerson

I returned to California to cover Liz Ryerson, a writer, artist, musician and game maker based in Berkeley. Header illustration and final illustration are by my partner in crime Irene Koh. All other material embedded was created by Liz's own fine hand. Liz's digital art is made using a tool called BECOME A GREAT ARTIST IN JUST TEN SECONDS! by Michael Brough and Andi McClure.

Berkeley, California, is a gentle old man; a retired monied Democrat reclining on dappled green hills. Swarming him are the upstart youth shrieking about wifi, chattering about newfound college promiscuity and skewed applications of decades-old philosophy to Ancient Greek literature, as if it'll do the Ancient Greeks any good.

It's an odd, sheltered, sickly optimistic world to live in, as if these fresh-skinned goofballs will contemplate for eternity which particular bohemian chick they are going to fuck next. This little leafy bubble of paradise is set with beautiful ornate 1930s cinemas and the dramatic architecture of the university – the only signs that someone ever knew what the hell they were doing in Berkeley. Because clearly, someone once knew what they were doing in Berkeley. If these kids would shut up for five seconds, they'd probably realise they've walked down the wrong street again.

I guess these are the people who run the world now, these earbudded, long-skirted, naive joymongers. They'll go straight to Google and make millions. I am jealous of them. They make me feel old. I often wonder what they do when it rains. But it never does here. It never rains in Berkeley.

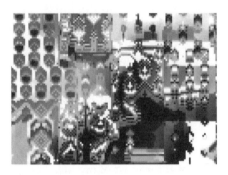

There are others, outside the young college-goers and thirty-something techbros, who quietly go about their existence making things on a shoestring. The artist, musician and <u>Problem Attic</u> creator Liz Ryerson lives down a leafy main street in Berkeley in half of a huge old house that smells, like most old houses in California do, of medicated timber. The downstairs, where we are staying, used to be the servants' quarters, so the kitchen takes over most of the ground floor. Nine people live in this side of the house. It is never quiet. I'm staying in a room that sleeps three – Liz's effervescent motormouth roommate Olivia is kindly giving me her mattress while she sleeps on the couch. It's a place with high ceilings, chunky old bathroom fixtures, and a sometime ant problem. I wake in the morning on my mattress (one of the best places to sleep I've had so far, perhaps apart from Harvey's loft, because it is flat and hard) and watch the tiny ombre insects make lines around my phone charger, crawl over my fingers. The sun is so strong through the blinds, scoring across the white walls patched together with hand-painted art, every surface in the room littered with beauty products and documents and clothes, it seems hard to be sad here.

But I know the secret is that everyone in California is profoundly sad. Sadness gets passed around like a blunt after sundown. No one talks about the drug. But it's there and it's messing everyone up. It gets in the lungs. California is the Wendy House state: it houses lost children who ran away from the violence of real life, a place where the promise is that you will never grow up. Dreams are not killed here; they are brought in in a coma state to be resuscitated, and sometimes they don't make it through the shock. Here I have been party to more sad stories of past lives than I've ever been party to, and I lived in the country of pissing-it-down, *Trainspotting*, and the corrosive cynicism represented on the BBC's *The Thick of It* for most of my life. The California way is to ignore the hardships. It's too nice here for dickishness. It's too good out for less than a smile and an only sometimes sincere 'Let's hang out'.

But days pass through this big creaking house that would never pass through a room in London; days in Berkeley are long and taste like buttered popcorn and soda water and sound like wind chimes and Joanna Newsom humming. At night, the sounds of Liz's next-door housemate squeaking in ecstasy mid-coitus are heard over the toilet flushing. Though I probably haven't been alone for more than an hour in three months, part of me loves the idea that each room in this house has some sort of noise emanating from it. Sometimes it's the sound of Liz's collection of Doom mods, sometimes it's the sharp low sound of Eartha Kitt's voice from next door. Sometimes we play Liz's music.

When the house moves, we move.

It feels like everyone is very determinedly living. It is comforting. And I think it is comforting to Liz, too. She was close to being homeless before I arrived, and was saved last minute by this huge rickety place with its breathing walls.

Originally from Gambier, Ohio, Liz had a troubled childhood she has often written about. It's obvious many societal labels have been pressed on her that she felt uncomfortable with, and it's given her a particular cynicism towards artistic categories or merit. She often addresses the question of what making things actually means to her identity, is vocally suspicious of words such as 'trans', 'queer', 'community', 'game'. She seems to shift uneasily under the weight of what each label implies when people try to apply them, partly because they bring assumptions and responsibilities that she feels have never truly served her. Liz's output is incredibly diverse: she has written in-depth game criticism for places such as Midnight Resistance, the New Statesman and Unwinnable, but she also makes the beautiful digital art that is throughout this essay, deeply architectural exploratory games, and atmospheric music. Perhaps she would even be uncomfortable with the label 'creator' or 'artist', but we will settle on the idea that she makes.

'I saw a quotation somewhere that said Jennifer Aniston's life is probably one hundred times more interesting than any character she plays,' Liz says, her legs curled under her on her bed. She has a shyness that makes her seem younger than she is, but when she articulates her ideas she's so intellectually expressive that you are aware that Liz's gentleness is providing a mask.

'You think of Hollywood actresses and you only think of them as these one-dimensional characters,' she continues, slowly, 'but in reality they're just these extremely complex people like everyone else. They're probably extremely interesting in the way that anyone can be really interesting. And that's the thing: media puts a mask over things. It puts a mask over everything, and we've come to see that mask as being really sexy, kind of the most interesting thing. Stylised and attractive, in a way. When you lift that mask, instead of getting more boring, people just get infinitely more complex and amazing and interesting, regardless of who they are, even if they are a construction worker or an actuary or something.'

I think about how this informs her outlook on life. The labels people use to describe her, particularly because they are often associated with a social minority, often have the effect of dismantling her complexity as a person, as they would anyone. When you remove any internet 'mask' from Liz, she becomes much deeper than you think. I once said to her that her game Problem Attic made me 'feel bad', like when I listen to The Cure's *Disintegration* – which is true. I do feel bad when I play Problem Attic, in a broad, lazy way, in a kind of unsettled, low-level existential way. I feel the same way when I listen to *Disintegration*. But the idea that someone might label something she made as making you 'feel bad' seems to sadden Liz, at the same time as she recognises that transmitting discomfort through games is hugely valuable and something that she aims to explore. She didn't mention when she wrote down my thoughts on Problem Attic making me 'feel bad' that, well, *Disintegration* is my favourite Cure album. It's the album of a personal, existential pain.

'When you're making stuff there's this huge level of complexity underneath every person. There's some sort of unified thing connecting it, existence,' she says. The sun is shining outside, and the ants are breezily wandering amongst our toes. 'The way that people think about themselves, the way that people exist, the sort of emotions that people have. So I think making art or something creative is essentially tapping into that. You don't need to be undergoing extreme circumstances to have extreme emotions: people experience that just walking around every day. It's not necessarily that people who are creative are experiencing more emotions than other people or are more sensitive to it. I just think there's something very mundane about the incredible complexity that's in everybody. There's something very complex about how mundane it is.'

She stumbles a little bit, and reconfigures what she is saying. 'If I make stuff I make stuff for random people. I don't make stuff to be cool, or be recognised as someone who is "cool and ahead of their time", or be recognised as someone who is, you know ... all that identity bullshit. It's making stuff to survive. Not just survive on a personal level but survive as a way of making sense of the other things that people are feeling or experiencing. There's something very boring about that, in a way that's not bad.'

One morning I woke up and Liz said, 'My friend said my game made someone throw up.'

(Pippin Barr was teaching Problem Attic to his students.)

I think I went through about four emotions: the first being amusement, the second being admiration (a game that can make you throw up? I thought they invented Oculus for that), the third dropping to concern, and finally, when I looked at how dismayed Liz was I felt her discomfort. She doesn't want to make people uncomfortable. Problem Attic transmits a particular feeling that not many people know how to interpret.

We have been playing Doom mods and listening to music and strolling around Berkeley all week in between my grappling with techbros in coffee shops. The Doom mods have been a trip deep into nostalgic wonderment for me: the mindfuck existential horror feel, the lo-fi grunginess of

Doom is intoxicating, the music in particular is something that puts me right back there in a state where I was craning to have my elbows sit on the desk because I was too small to reach the computer. Everything in Doom seemed satanic then. Like a witch had made it. Loading it up was like peering into the forbidden dimensions. Doom was ugly-pretty then, but now it is just beautiful.

Liz has never really left Doom in a way. She entered games through an appreciation of another's interests, or perhaps through an interest in participation, and the online social linchpin was Wolfenstein 3D and Doom mods.

'My first online friend was this guy Chris, who I still talk to occasionally,' Liz explains, as she rifles through her early music compositions – arrangements of old Mario soundtracks, some incredibly competent-sounding work for something that was composed when she was only fourteen. 'He's just really wacky and has lots of ideas.' Liz smiles. 'Very outgoing and weird. He kind of encouraged me to do a lot of different stuff. I realised how important that was for me at that particular time. That I had a weird friend who encouraged me with it. We'd send emails back and forth, and he'd be talking about Wolfenstein or Doom levels or making music. I'd gotten into Radiohead at that point so I was sending him impressions of *Kid A*, and that was a lot of fun. I made Wolfenstein levels and it instilled in me the importance of community: I was like, I'm going to make the best mod *ever*.

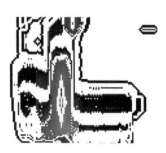

'There was one guy who probably has all the Wolf3D levels ever made on his website since '96 or '95, and it's still up! And it looks exactly the same as it did back then. It looks exactly the same as it did in 1998. And he still updates it too! That guy is responsible for any kind of community for user-made Wolf levels. The Doom community was bigger because it was easier to make mods [without copyright infringing]. Actually you can download my Wolf3D mod for free even though you're not supposed to – it just never got popular enough that anyone cared.'

If Liz had never been interested in talking to Chris, I think, perhaps she would never have slipped into the dark worlds iD Software had created. Is creation about connection? When we think about Auteur theory, are we just kidding ourselves that one person alone is the genius? Perhaps the need to need other people is actually at the core of creation. The need to be needed. The need to be wanted. The need to say something through something.

'I definitely was very isolated when I grew up,' Liz says to me. 'Even the few friends that I had were tremendously helpful for me in figuring out who I was and developing my own sense of self.'

I feel like the same can be said for the creative self. I personally never knew who I was on paper until my more talented friends started to ask.

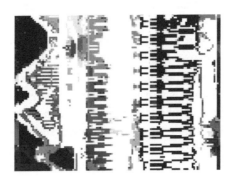

'That's the first time anyone's really told me I should be doing something with my music,' Liz tells me, when we walk through the UC Berkeley grounds. 'When you said that.' She is talking about my reaction to the music she is making. She is a talented electronic music composer. Her recent work includes tracks for Mirrormoon EP; hers are tempered, atmospheric, evocative.

Part of me is upset, nervous about this. The idea that I might be putting an emphasis on her. The idea that I might be changing her idea of who she is. Since the beginning of this project there have been a lot of issues I've worried about. There's the idea that I am including some people and excluding others; the idea that I might be making a 'canon' if one could ever be so egotistical as to think what you're doing is relevant; the anxiety, sometimes guilt, over my distance to the people I am writing about. If there is any distance at all when I arrive, there isn't by the time I have left and it bothers me.

The people I choose to write about are those I personally want to know more about and want to tell others about, but they also have to be people whom I've met at least once and feel like I can trust. It might seem like something Hunter S. Thompson wouldn't worry about, but in previous hallucinogenic *The Beach*-esque travels I've stayed on couches in situations where I thought it might not be outrageous to consider being woken by a stab to the chest, or being raped. Even these are things I think about when I choose who to stay with, not that anything so extreme should really weigh on my mind for longer than a few seconds. They are just game developers.

But what I always worry about the most is the thing that is probably analogous to the *Star Trek* Prime Directive – stay with me now – that only my interviewees are the ones with 'superior technology' and I'm some silent, informational sponge that takes up space in their house and writes down what sort of shower gel they use. The idea that my very presence might be changing the people I'm writing about, even in subtle ways, is a perma-anxiety.

Of concern: are they performing for me? Are they performing who they want to be? Did Tim Rogers, who lives only a few miles away from here, plan for me to write about his Gibson, rainbow-colour dinosaur jumper, late-night Japan melancholy? Did Katharine Neil want me to admire her reckless attitude towards marriage-for-money, did she plan to have my piece be as political as possible? Am I some sort of manipulated pawn? Who are they? Did I even know them? Did I know them well enough? Tim seems uninterested in my return to California. Harvey Smith seems sad I left Lyon. I can't remember what London looks like sometimes.

Harvey. Harvey told me to watch *Almost Famous* and it really fucked with me. 'Watch it,' he said. 'You'll like it.'

What am I going to do with this anxiety?

*

The late Phillip Seymour Hoffman's Lester Bangs sits there in *Almost Famous* and says to the main character, 'Oh man. You made friends with them. Friendship is the booze they feed ya. They want you to get drunk on feeling like you belong.' But then immediately afterwards he contradicts himself. 'Because great art is about guilt, and longing, and love disguised as sex and sex disguised as love.' In order to be able to write well, the guilt, doesn't it have to exist as in the art? If great art is about the closeness, the proximity to a subject, what the fuck are we all doing trying to maintain a distance from it when we write about it? I guess maybe you'd have to have an argument with yourself about whether criticism or gonzo journalism or interviewing or whatever the hell I'm doing here is an 'art' (I mean, it's probably not and I don't know what it might be), but I am laying this all out here because I think I'm having a meltdown.

'The only true currency is what you share with someone when you're uncool.' Again, Lester, Cameron Crowe, whatever, doesn't this require that I get closer to the subjects rather than far away? I want to be around when they're uncool. I want to be around when they're fucked up. I'm always home, too, Lester Bangs; I'm at home on whoever's couch. I'm uncool. None of my clothes have been washed. I've worn the same clothes to sleep and to wake. You are scorching the pavements outside, Berkeley, and all I've got are these faux-leather pants that were too cold in Berlin, and now I have to walk to Trader Joe's in them. Why did I even bring the faux-leather pants? This is the uncool part of me. The part that is too damn hot and really darned sticky and never smells good.

I want my interviewees to know they make worthwhile things, and want them to go on to make fucking astounding things. But the idea that I might be warping or changing the path of it by giving my feedback, by encouraging or by advertising, rather than just observing it take place is strange. I am finally making my peace with this now, as I write this. Because I understand that just like any other thing I write as a critic, I am part of a process, and none of the process is objective. If I have to tell Liz her music provokes the flashing lights in my skull so be it. I'm here now. Entertain me.

The significant factor of support, the sort of support I worry about now, in the creation of Liz's work is something that we end up talking about often. The idea of 'support', not just from players, listeners, 'consumers', but support from people who know what they are doing when they make something. Liz's music is obviously good, and I feel like she should be receiving encouragement for it. She has composed tracks for <u>Mirror Moon EP</u>, <u>Crypt Worlds</u> and Anna Anthropy's landmark game <u>Dys4ia</u>. She is currently composing a bonus track for <u>Videoball</u>.

Part of the problem, Liz says to me as we walk the weed-fogged streets of Berkeley, eyes stinging, is that in order to have the motivation to create, you have to surround yourself with people who encourage you to do so. Sometimes those people have to be people who you trust have the authority to tell you what you make is good.

Liz cites moving in with prolific game creator <u>Anna Anthropy</u> and her then partner <u>Daphny David</u> as a moment when she realised she had the encouragement she needed to make music, art and games. She was surrounded by people who were already doing these things. She had no excuse not to create. Others wondered why she wasn't.

'When somebody makes something weird, people tend to associate it with that individual,' Liz says to me, the sound of chattering and cooking sounding through the house as we sit under blankets. 'That it's a sort of crazy brain that formulates these things, forges them out of nothing. But that's really not the case at all, it's just that some people are more attuned to frequencies maybe, or maybe some want to explore it. But it's all a thing that exists, and it's not just a creation of an individual. It's a very American thing to view entire artworks as the creation of one person.

'It's really depressing to be a person and sit by yourself and try and create entirely within yourself. Sometimes that can be a good thing to do, but after a while you just get really depressed and there's nowhere you can go. You need other people to bring something into that. You need other people to force you into those situations. But a lot of game developers, especially coders, don't have to be forced into that situation where they have that kind of life experience, where they are actively in conflict or, not even in conflict but just trying to communicate with someone else. You know it's like a competitive mindset, and I think I was sort of trained to think this way too, where it "ruins your internal purity or something" as far as creative things go. It's not been that way at all. It's just opened creative things up. I appreciate a lot of things that I didn't before. Other people can definitely have a negative impact on things – there are times when it can be really overwhelming – but I think it's really important to have other people to interact with in person.'

Liz has become renowned for being 'unaccommodating' artistically, almost as if there is an accusation that she is being deliberately obtuse with everything she does, much in the manner that Katharine Neil might feel about how she is regarded by the games 'establishment' now, or in the way that the internet thinks that Tim Rogers is an 'invented' person (something that people said to me after I wrote the essay). It is becoming more obvious than ever that the people who are willing to drive a spike-loaded monster truck through cultural norms and take the consequences are those who understand how art speaks to people, and more importantly, why it speaks to them.

When Liz sits down to make a game, such as the isometric exploration game Responsibilities, which she made for Ludum Dare with Andi McClure, or the more recent anti-platformer Problem Attic, there's a particular thing she is looking to convey, rather than to correspond with many ideas about what a 'game' might be.

'I'm trying to create a feeling or a mood and using the available tools rather than saying, "I am going to make a game",' she explains one night. 'You know, because when people say they are going to make "a game" there are explicit things that you are supposed to do. Like "you better make sure that players know what they are doing". People say that Problem Attic is very confusing, but there's only a few buttons that you ever use. Yes, functionality does change, but it's very clear what the controls are and all that kind of stuff, the rest of the stuff is what's unclear.

'But, you know, I like the idea of getting lost or confused in a videogame space and finally figuring out where to go, because the amount of time you spent in that space confused is time you spent building a relationship with the space. It hasn't really been pleasurable at all, but because of the way that the market for games work the worst that you could do – or at least this is what the research says – the worst thing you could do is confuse someone to the point of them quitting. And if that happens they get frustrated, they won't like it, they won't pay for it, they'll get mad. So it's this self-reinforcing loop, where people can't take any degree of pain when they're playing a game or watching a movie or listening to music. They are reacting to this initial pain.'

She expands this idea further. 'With games it reminds me of this article about how different countries train their children: in the US, people take so many safety precautions. They don't want their kids to get scraped knees. In a lot of other countries they let kids make those mistakes within a certain degree. That really helps because it trains basic behaviour and things you will be experiencing in life. There's this sense that parents are so afraid of their children growing up and going into the world. I had a cousin who broke his arm when he fell, but thing is, when you're still developing, that kind of stuff, you know, it heals really quickly. Our bodies are intentionally that way. It's better to allow people freedom, because then you can feel like you're not talking down to them. If you don't give people freedom you're not allowing them to develop their own sort of relationship with something. It's all just being defined by you.'

But her work's relationship with the player is the thing she is primarily interested in. 'It's not just a manifesto sort of idea. It's that information is better communicated that way when you're using those tools. If you're trying to teach something by telling them something or writing it down, then that's one thing, but if you're making a game to try and teach something, and you put in text, or you put in something explicit, you take something out of that experience.

'Not everything is meant to be understood or appreciated

right away. It can be a lot easier if you're prepared to go into something with that mindset. This is why I don't like the idea that you have to keep players entertained, because that way there's this constant revenue source. I think it's really important to have a beginning and an end. Because in the end "this did value my time": regardless of whether it took a long time to play through, it didn't just keep putting the carrot further and further away.'

I keep pushing Liz to tell me more about her music, something she started to make because she wanted to make soundtracks for her mods. She used to follow John Romero's webpage and he posted about OC Remix, a videogame music community that hosts free fan arrangements of music. When she turned fifteen she was using a programme called Modplug, which is a free programme, called a tracker, something used to compose for Amiga or C64, and it puts the notes into what looks like a spreadsheet.

'I found samples online and I made this thing which is an arrangement of something from Super Mario RPG,' Liz explains. 'I played in orchestra, I played cello. I played piano for a while but I didn't like it because you couldn't play in between the notes. So I knew basic skills but I didn't know music theory – I knew enough to pick up on stuff. I made midis to put in my Wolfenstein mod. I always wanted to make music, and I used to not have friends and I had a bunch of cassette tapes that I'd listen to over and over again.'

Liz is contemplating moving from Berkeley to Brooklyn, New York. The more I tell her that she should be making more music, the more she realises that there isn't an electronic music community near her that she can find the support from. And we both know the value of the company of people who make things. I'm afraid and excited for her. I don't know what she will do next, but I know I want to hear about it. I know I want to listen to it.

We sit, again, at Pepples Donut Farm, dissecting donuts,

or 'doughnuts' if you are British. Irene Koh is drawing us as we talk about our favourite comedians: Bill Hicks and Eddie Izzard. All of a sudden Liz says to me: 'You know when I was young, I used to go for long walks. And I never came back the same way. I like to come back a different way.'

Donut by Irene Koh

Embed with ...
Brendon Chung

I escaped to LA to stay with Brendon Chung, who is the centre of a small group of developers who work together in a space called Glitch City LA. Brendon makes, under the guise of 'Blendo Games', some of the most interesting PC games in our PCscape. Fellow Glitcher and Hyper Light Drifter guy Teddy Diefenbach was my stringer.

I got out of E3 like Dufresne out of shit and went straight to Glitch City Los Angeles to bathe in something that hasn't got the stink of commercialism all over it, and it was there in all its post-E3 glory: Glitch City Demo Night II.

A night of diverse people talking about their inspirations and giving advice, held in their little venue off West Washington Boulevard in Culver City. The lights are dim, the people are mild and friendly, IGF Chairman Brandon Boyer slinks in the back with a glint in his eye and a melting half-smile like something good is going to happen. Talks that are five minutes long, are positive, and don't sell anything. Fuck selling anything for now. There's beer, and later the Indiecade afterparty.

The speakers are heartfelt, charismatic even, the last three in particular illustrating something I see so little of through the lens of the games press. Game creators have talents that aren't just making games, and producing them can be the least important aspect of who they are. They are bringing what they learn from the arts in other areas to make their work spectacular.

It is easier to see people as people here, in this space. It's easier to look at people within a broader context, as people who live in a broader culture. They aren't just this one obsession. Your life does not need to be in an eternal wrassle with the concept or purity of the word 'game' in order to produce something good. Here games seem less the obsessive-compulsive burden of one person, but the shared process of people supporting each other.

Glitch City banner for the Demo Night

The third-to-last speaker Lisa Brown, for example, radiates a kind of energy that if you tried to ignore it would just sneak up and noogie you. A designer at Insomniac Games, she also spends time on smaller projects at Glitch City. Glitch City isn't just a place for people who consider themselves 'indie', but a place for people who share similar values of artistic cross-pollination.

Not only is Lisa an excellent presenter, she's also capable of adorable, emotive illustrations, and sometimes those illustrations include the level design dragon that lives in her brain.

Nina Freeman, visiting from New York, presented a talk on vignette games. For her, vignette games are an extension of poetry, her first love, and she reads out her favourite poem. Games that can paint mood or feeling are important to her.

Though he's known primarily for his work programming Hyper Light Drifter, Teddy Diefenbach is a trained singer and studied music. To finish the night, he wrote a song about his anguish reading internet comments on his solo game project, Kyoto Wild, and then sung it to the Glitch

City crowd. Though I've known Teddy for years, since we met as Conference Associates at our first Game Developers Conference, I never knew he could sing quite like this.

The shared cooperative studio space at Glitch City isn't a unique idea, but it does play host to game creators who go out of their way to be welcoming and support a community – not just of game developers, but any kind of creator. After it was formed a year ago, it was an accident that the community was populated with people who primarily make games, but the space welcomes any kind of artist. 'Glitch Knitty', for example, is an event that happened in the Glitch City space on the twentieth of April. People were invited to come to knit, crochet and cross-stitch together.

There's a healthy diet of not-videogames going on. This will become the most pleasant realisation, one that happens over and over, for the next two weeks.

Brendon Chung, better known on the internet as Blendo Games, is the talented, unmurdery Godfather of Glitch City LA. I know this because Teddy tells me when I arrive, 'If you know Brendon, you get in. All you need to do is know Brendon.'

I got in because of Teddy, so that's the first thing you need to know. That Teddy isn't always right.

The second thing you need to know is that I wanted to write about Brendon. This isn't because I thought Teddy is uninteresting (he's making two games at once, can programme like a motherfucker, is trying to make a game that approximates Bushido Blade and he might do it, he can sing R&B better than almost any man I have ever met). It isn't because I didn't think anyone else at Glitch wasn't worthy of attention. It's because I had never met Brendon, and didn't know anything about Brendon apart from that he made Thirty Flights Of Loving, one of my favourite games. You have to indulge your own curiosity sometimes.

Brendon is currently making a game called Quadrilateral

Cowboy out of Glitch City, and, along with other founding members of Glitch City such as Ben Esposito (Unfinished Swan), Alex Preston (Hyper Light Drifter), and Seiji Tanaka (TURBOCATS), is primarily responsible for bringing people together here. It's on a very wide quiet street in Culver City. The ceiling is pinned with large squares of yellow and grey fabric that give the workspace a tent-like feel. It is cool and quiet inside, and (this is important to a Scottish writer) has tea and coffee-making facilities.

It also has a bathroom that has been painted with blackboard paint and is provided with large stubs of pastel-colour chalk.

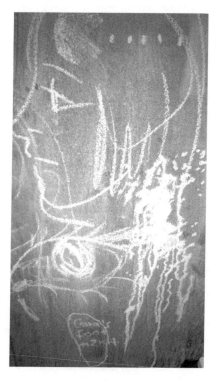

Cara's foot 2k14

(I am left to wonder for a while how it is possible that it is not populated with various fancy drawings of phalluses, but Brendon tells me later that this is because they instituted an early ban. 'Pretty quickly we had to enact the no-penis rule, because it was getting out of control,' he explains. 'It was blossoming out of penises ... Okay, guys, very funny, it's on a motorcycle, it's eating cereal, it's doing all these things, very funny.')

A week later, all I have done is sit quietly in Glitch City silently cursing my broken baby, a MacBook with a malfunctioning hard disk drive cable. It is strange to have your only lifeline to the world be unresponsive, sitting there in silver shame, attempting to avoid my recriminating stares, and me cheating on it with a Chromebook. Brendon has been quietly modelling new objects for Quadrilateral Cowboy, which is his new project. I think I'd fallen in love with it before I ever played it. He tells me later one of his favourite filmmakers is Robert Rodriguez, and it all makes sense. Their DIY aesthetic is in tune.

It is a game Brendon calls twentieth-century cyberpunk. There are a number of 'jobs' you can undertake: something to steal, something to find, and you have a suitcase deck to hack switches, or a little remote robot on legs to do your bidding.

But instead of the worn neon *Bladerunner* cyberpunk universe, it is a square, classically Blendo Games-style universe in the vein of Thirty Flights Of Loving and Gravity Bone, his previous games. Things are often in sepia tones, cassette tapes lie around; there's a refined, almost screwball comedy feeling to the game – though the main characters are all women and they do not talk. There is a strong feeling of the working class around Quadrilateral Cowboy, an emphasis on what hands do, make and use. Objects feel solid; when you connect wires to hack something, twentieth-century style, they do so with a satisfying reel and click, the keys of your suitcase deck sound like they respond to your instructions with the whole of their thickness. It's like you are in a quirky heist movie directed by Hitchcock, but Dr Emmett Brown from *Back to the Future* has given you your tools.

It is relaxing; at its heart it is a puzzle game that never punishes you for experimenting or making mistakes. It is about the joy of putting a set of instructions in and getting something spectacular out. It can make anyone feel like a hacker.

In fact, Quadrilateral Cowboy is a game so flexible in terms of what you can do with it that other people can get carried away with their experiments. One afternoon in Glitch City Teddy was procrastinating work on Hyper Light Drifter, and attempted to get the computer in Quadrilateral Cowboy to produce a series of beeps approximating a pop song.

It turned out not bad.

Brendon does live development streams every so often: he is very open about letting people see the inside of his code.

Part of me wonders if Brendon is very open about how he overcomes development problems because he, like me, grew up a PC gamer, in internet communities where knowledge of how to make things was not proprietary. Where conversations were often hostile but never uninteresting, where the extraction of what and why were important. Where Quake II ruled the world. (We play Quake II one afternoon at Glitch City; it has never lost its thrill.)

One night we go to dinner in a nice place in Culver City annoyingly named 'Lyfe Kitchen'. 'How did Glitch City start?' I ask Brendon, wondering if I can vandalise the 'y' out of 'Lyfe' on the front of the restaurant. In fact, perhaps the whole name.

'So I started with [a work group called] Strawberry Jam,' he explains. 'Every Sunday, a group of us would meet at a coffee shop and we would bring our laptops, and just start working. And we liked it. Because it meant we were out of our houses. It meant we had to wear clothes. It meant we had to smell okay.'

I laugh in the way that only freelance writers can laugh at this statement.

'We were thinking, why don't we do Strawberry Jam more often instead of trying to bum a table every time?' he continues. 'So then some of the guys started actively searching. It was two groups of people, and Ben Esposito was the common bond [between] the two groups and brought the two groups together. That's when I met Casey Hunt and Alex Preston. And we were looking for a place, we found one in Downtown, which was scary and was in a bad part of town, then we found Glitch City.'

'And it happened to be across the street from the best burger place in LA,' I say.

Brendon's voice goes all low and surreptitious. 'It was, uh, a very good location. And Pinches' tacos ... We have a lot of tacos. I don't know if you've noticed.'

I have been eating tacos for lunch every day since I got here.

It's Teddy's birthday halfway through my stay here; I buy him the last copy of Deadly Premonition: Director's Cut from the Gamestop near Brendon's house. We buy beer and I laugh at almost every reaction Brendon and Teddy have at the game – it is extraordinary, as if David Lynch made a game – and with the leftover beer the next night, I sit with Brendon on the couch and interrogate him about his thoughts on making things.

Brendon Chung is easy in manner, mostly a quiet, unassuming and amiable person. Something both frustrating and wonderful about him is that you know that a good library of films and books sits in his head and he is keeping all of their secrets until he needs them for his work, and then it goes into whatever game he is making. He rarely starts conversations, but he seems to like having them. It is natural for Brendon to think that games sit in a cultural spectrum like every other medium. He grew up in Los Angeles, where everyone, whether they want to or not, is exposed to movies, and his whole family is creative.

'My mom played a lot of music when she was younger,' Brendon explains to me. 'My dad liked drawing stuff when he was younger. My brother was film inclined. My sister works in graphic design.'

Brendon made his first game in elementary school in QBasic, and he's always been interested in games, but his need to make games never seemed like the only strand running through everything. He went to film school in San Diego; he's made films he's proud of.

He says when he began work at the late AAA game studio Pandemic here in LA, before they closed and he went solo, he found that everyone else was cross-disciplinary too. One of his teammates was an ex-TV cameraman, for example. Here in Glitch City, Teddy Diefenbach also has a film background; the same for Casey Hunt, who also works on Hyper Light Drifter.

For Brendon, making things seems like something necessary for him, but it doesn't really matter what medium they are in as long as he can keep making connections with people.

'There is something about having people play your stuff, enjoy your stuff,' he says to me. 'Knowing that you're making some sort of connection out there. For me, I love when someone makes something just for me. There are some movies out there that I think, you made this just for me. You made this movie to appeal straight to my senses. I like to try to make stuff for people who don't have stuff made for them.

'Gravity Bone was my attempt at "Can I make a story game?" It still had a lot of janky platforming and missions and objectives. But for Thirty Flights Of Loving I would try to make Gravity Bone but without traditional gameplay things. Can I just make this thing that is purely about "feel a certain thing", make a certain mood in the world? Is that enough to make this something that someone will enjoy? Because not everyone likes shooting things ... The idea is: what if it was nothing but mood? Cut out exposition, cut out objectives, cut out everything that games do.'

'There's no dialogue in your games,' I say.

'Yeah. Other games do it. I don't like competing against other people. I'm not going to win against Planescape: Torment, or Bioware, whatever they do,' Brendon replies.

'Games are an underestimated means of telling a story,' I say. 'You can tell a story in a game just by making an action available.'

Brendon nods. 'The onus is on the player to be the thing that drives things forward. Something that's important for me in story is that not everyone likes story, so it's important to me that if you don't like story you can skip all of it or most of it. When I play games I skip past text bubbles because they don't generally interest me, so games like Thirty Flights or Gone Home, if you want you can totally speed run it. For me, what irks me is when games force you to read every precious word or cutscene which I don't ever want to do.'

I ask if there's a particular game that affected his outlook.

'The huge inspiration for me was Another World by Eric Chahi,' he says. 'It's really interesting. It's called Another World in Europe, Out Of This World in America. It's a side-scrolling game but it's told with zero words, and the art is very vector-based. It's made by one guy, and the gag is that he just started making this game, a scientist in a laboratory gets zapped by his own experiment and gets teleported to another universe, and that he made this first sequence as he went along. The game has this feeling of spontaneity, like he has no idea, that kind of energy. It's amazing – like, now you're in a death arena, now you're in a ... It's just amazing.'

'Thirty Flights has that feeling,' I say, 'of … you know when Raymond Chandler says when you've run out of stuff to say, have a man come through the door with a gun? Thirty Flights is the same – it doesn't waste any time. It never occurred to me that you could literally move the player, just do a jump cut.'

'In college I was a film student,' Brendon says. 'I love movies, I like watching them and I like making them. But games, we talked about this [we'd talked in the car about how we hate that games' only cinematic takeaway is cut scenes] – they take this movie stuff and you're like, well, great. But you want them to use it in a different way, I guess. For me I wanted to use movie stuff without pausing a game, without making players watch a cut scene. What if you could integrate them seamlessly while you're playing – you can leave your hands on the controllers and you'll be okay. So that's the kind of approach I try to take with that.'

'Are you a storyteller?' I ask him.

'I worked in AAA for a while,' he begins. 'And the company I worked for [Pandemic], they made really bold choices in things, but as the company got bigger and bigger and bigger, I felt the company started specialising in the same thing over and over again. I've always been interested in storytelling, like at elementary school and making shitty Doom mods and Quake mods – so for me it's near and dear to my heart. But I don't want to be the guy that does story stuff. That's why the first thing I did was not story stuff – like Flotilla and Atom Zombie Smasher. Because I find it more interesting to do something you're terrible at, because the results are more interesting.'

'Why don't you develop for consoles?' I ask.

'There's something about console development that's super cumbersome,' he says.

'Closed?'

'Yeah, there's all this paperwork you have to do.'

'The PC seems so egalitarian, so open. You can distribute

93

games for free,' I say.

'When you say open ...' Brendon nods. 'It's also ... the files are just sitting there. You can just click on them. You can just click into the directory and see what all the files are doing. Like I was playing Farcry 3, and there are some things I didn't quite agree with, and some people out there went ahead and modified the files to remove the mini map or whatever. And that's a thing you can do here. I think that's great.'

'Quadrilateral Cowboy is very nostalgic for that era of the PC games command line.'

'I mean, that's the era I grew up in. Messing around with autoconfig. Trying to make this stupid game work on my computer.' Brendon smiles.

'There's a romanticisation in my head about the jankiness of getting computer games to work,' I say. 'I had an ATI Rage graphics card that never worked. It shaped my ability to play games because some things didn't work, and some things did. For example, Mechwarrior 2 loaded. But P.O.D. never loaded. Mechwarrior 2 wasn't an *amazing* game, but there's a tiny shard of wonder left in me for that game just because it loaded.'

'If you asked me at the time I would have said I hated it and just wanted it to work,' Brendon says, 'but looking back on it as that Dwarf Fortress feel – you've gotta *earn* your fun. You gotta fight your way through.'

Brendon's bookshelves

I guess I'm in love with Brendon's bookshelves. There's such a huge variety of stuff there. Not just science fiction and pulp, but instruction manuals, *The Grammar of Architecture*, a book on the history of Chinese and Japanese civilisations, a whole host of Prima strategy guides, Michael Chabon, C# manual next to Mark Twain.

I love personal libraries because it is like opening up someone's brain and having a look inside. These pictures are the inside of Brendon's brain. And it has a lot of stuff going on.

Love Something

'Why are games special?' I ask Brendon. '*Are* they special?'

'For me it's not about where videogames are right now,' he says, reclining further into the Glitch City couch. 'More like what we could do with videogames. We play these games right now and they do things, but it's that feeling ... We are at that stage in film where you just see the train coming towards you and people are freaking out because they think they're going to be run over by the train. Just thinking about where we're going to be in twenty years – games are going to be freaking crazy. There's something about that that is really exciting.'

Part of me wonders that if film were easier to get into would games lose Brendon completely. Actually, I know we wouldn't. His bookshelves are full of Prima guides and C# manuals – he's the Tarantino of videogames. But he tells me that if it were easier to live as a film director he might have done more of it.

'I like being able to pay for my roof,' Brendon says. 'I really want to do videogames, and I am really interested in doing film stuff. But I couldn't ever figure out how to make a living doing film and video projects. I was pretty confident about the games: you make a game and then you sell it directly to people, it's digital. But with film I felt with some practice I could eventually make something good, but there wasn't any direct way to sell it. Like, do I sell it to a studio, do I put it on YouTube? How does this work? I had no idea.'

Perhaps there are some ways in which games are winning – that is, our young auteurs. They have a way to sell their work directly to the people who want it. They hold the sweat of their own brow.

'It is okay to make a living off what you're making,' Brendon says, assuredly. 'There are some developers out there who think it dilutes the art, making people pay money for your thing, or doing some sort of financial transaction for your art.

'And if you're an artist and I like your work, I want you to continue making your work. And you're not going to be able to do that if you don't have some attempt at asking for something. It's nothing to be ashamed of: to be able to put food in your mouth and pay for your rent. I hope that becomes more accepted.'

*

The intimation is always that I should hate Los Angeles. When I came here before, I always assumed that there was something I was missing that would show LA to be some sort of cheap drunk tarted up on the sort of nail polish that stains your nails orange, a city where the movies and the lyrics of Hole's 'Celebrity Skin' push all griminess to the surface so you can see it.

But this has not been my experience any time I have come here. I spent all my time in Culver City and Hollywood this time, and I always thought I'd hate LA, I always thought I'd come away with a thin filthy layer of it on me. Everyone outside LA gripes that it is shallow and awful, that people value terrible things here. Perhaps I don't hang out with the right people. I never hang out with the right people. Or maybe I always hang out with the right people. Maybe, out of all of my excruciating flaws, this is my one redeeming virtue.

I went to dinner with the writer Tom Bissell, who is writing some big-budget blockbuster game as is his wont, the sort of thing I never play any more. We sat there and looked over at the sunset on the Hollywood Hills. Later he'd tell me I fall in love with the wrong people, and he's right, he's right, but you never know how you feel about something until you've had to live there. You go there and you live there and then you work out what it is later.

When I first got here I got hit on by a fedora-wearing movie director of some documentary in a rooftop bar in Downtown LA. Teddy said this was the one true Los Angeles experience that I'd had. I only thought: it seems like there's a lot of acceptance for strangeness, difference here. As if the whole of Los Angeles is just, in itself, a museum of personalities, of eccentricities. As if it is just Brendon Chung's eclectic collection of weird and wonderful books. It just opens at the movie page more often than not. And I think in the hands of someone smart, that book can make really great games.

A Brendon sketch

Embed with ...
Nina Freeman

I went to Brooklyn, New York, to visit Nina Freeman, who is currently making a game called Cibele. It is an autobiographical game about Nina's experience of having sex for the first time with someone she met through an online game. The game uses real filmed sequences and sections of an MMO-like game to tell an emotionally difficult story, one of flirtation and betrayal. The art from the game, made by Rebekka Dunlap, is interspersed throughout this article. The header image of Nina was lovingly drawn by New York-based illustrator Elizabeth Simins.

We sit slumped, side by side, close to each other, in Nina Freeman's Brooklyn apartment. We are pre-game drunk. It is too hot. We can't afford to put the air conditioning on. Our skin has a glazed sheen. We wear the least amount of clothes possible.

It's smothering, like sleeping restless between tropical sheets, Williamsburg presses humid fingers on our thighs, and we are gazing at Usher.

We say nothing, we do nothing, our hands are limp on the couch. He is singing about how no one kisses like us. Nina's long-term boyfriend Emmett is due to come home tonight – high cheekbones, broad shoulders, handsome grin – and I can feel the tension try to dissipate from this fact. I am jealous of her real estate, terraces and terraces of 'this part is mine'. The last time I had sex the weather was hot but at least there was no exhausting humidity. The last time I had sex seems like a Grand Canyon away because the man in the video should stop dancing.

Usher is shirtless, purrs on the screen. The video tempts us by cutting away. He touches his body when he dances to suggest we cannot.

I think about what Nina is thinking. I think about whether Nina is thinking about Usher like I am thinking about Usher. I am thinking about whether she is thinking about how our sexuality is being manipulated by this video. Does Usher know he is binding us up like a thread around a finger? I want him to know exactly how. I want him to receive push notifications. Objectifying notifications. I want him to get mindfuck notifications that vibrate his phone off the table every time we think something filthy about this video. I want him to know that Nina Freeman and I are sitting here mindfucking him, weak from the New York heat. I know Nina is thinking this way because Emmett has been away, and in this weather we have mostly been talking about How We Like It, games and otherwise. She has lent me a book entitled *The Ethical Slut*.

I guess Nina is famous for making games about sexuality by now, or she should be, but this new game she is making – Cibele – it has been playing with me rather than me playing with it. I have come to understand very quickly that Nina and

I are very similar. Our obsessions with the personal being important. The lists of men we might make fuckplans about. Our opinions about emotional terrorism. Our experiences in teaching. Our backgrounds in poetry and literature. Our anxieties about being a woman, being ambitious, punching a hole through the grip of an industry moulded like men want it. It has become a sort of joke in my head. We feel small and alone and we make things that we want to make to feel big. Later we'd sit in a sake bar pulling our hair and poring over the war map of an industry that finds us inscrutable.

'Usher would get it,' I conclude. It seems like a feeble statement. So I say it again. 'Usher would get it.'

Nina laughs.

Screenshot from Cibele. Nina plays the main character.
Samantha Corey is the filmmaker.

Nina Freeman has it together. She programs and designs all her own games, of which there are eight, and she is working on the ninth, Cibele. She owns two hentai pillows and is prone to showing me beautiful things that look like they come from a fairyland and saying, 'This is my whole aesthetic.'

She shows me this Grimes video and says, 'This is my whole aesthetic.'

Nina has recently become popular enough to receive death threats for her game How Do You Do It, a short game about her girlhood experiences attempting to figure out how sex works via Barbie dolls. You know you are a woman who said something interesting on the internet when you receive death threats. It is like graduating, but instead of smiling at your parents you cry to your pillow for several weeks when no one is around and contemplate your own worthlessness until you get angry and creative and emerge some sort of burning, fuschine dragon. Nina wrote an article on designing thoughtful games about sex and relationships just a few days later:

'It doesn't matter if you think sex doesn't belong in games, because sex is one of those basic human drives that manifests itself in our lives and in our art, whether by our own volition or in the minds of our players. Barbie dolls were not necessarily meant to be used as objects of sexual experimentation – but that didn't stop me when I was ten years old. Instead of ignoring sex in games, especially in games that are marketed to younger people, we should think about what we are saying already, and what we could be saying if we were more thoughtful.'

a person passes through history on a google search for truth
meanwhile i walk around soho
which is always like super models–
cut to me oblivious
in a sailor moon crop top

...

and one time i was playing sex with ken
until by accident i ripped ken's leg off
which kind of killed the mood

i was in aol cybersex chat rooms before i knew what sex
was

now i know even less about it
my bedroom is an anime bachelor pad
and here i am drinking a cocktail called
'the corpse reviver #2'

i hereby apologize to anyone and everyone i have ever
kissed

namaste

From <u>Untitled</u> by Nina Freeman

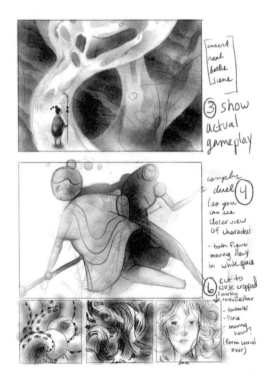

Nina has a degree in English Literature and a Masters of Science in Integrated Digital Media. Her first love was poetry, which has given birth to her love of 'vignette games'; games that are a snapshot of a feeling or moment, games that capture life in one small pinch of time and space. She cites my favourite, Stephen Lavelle's Slave Of God, as a good example, and she taught my vignette game Sacrilege to a packed class at Code Liberation. Nina has made a number of vignettes, including Ladylike, her most recent. Nina's last two games are interpretations of real things that happened to her.

I ask her why it is important to her to make games.

'I'm sort of obsessed with becoming renowned,' she tells me, as we regard each other over a flickering candle at a dim little Williamsburg izakaya. 'Both my parents, who are divorced so it was mostly my mom, would never recognise anything I did. Once in a while they did, but when it was something I was really proud of I would be like, "Mom, I did this thing, I wrote this poem and it got into some magazine at school ..." It was never a big deal to her. And I think part of that was her being bad at expressing that kind of emotion. But I didn't know that as a kid so I was obsessed with finding the one thing that would impress her. I've just grown into that. It's become my personality. I'm never really satisfied with anything I do. Nothing ever seems like it's good enough for anyone in my mind. Even if my mom does praise me it still doesn't feel complete for some reason.'

'You talked last night about the fact that creating things gave you control over things,' I say.

'Yeah,' Nina says. 'I feel like [my mom] would have been impressed if I'd pursued things she'd impressed upon me like acting. But those things weren't giving me the sense of accomplishment programming and making games do.

'When I realised "Poetry gives me a sense of control, I can express myself in this way, people are praising me for it outside of my family", that was a good adrenaline rush.

But it's a drug. It only lasts for so long. I keep having to make more and more stuff to get that short-term feeling of accomplishment.'

i opened up a microsoft word document
clippy krumped onto the screen–
'fucking hipster,' he sneered

From Untitled by Nina Freeman

'What do you like about sex the most?' I ask Nina.

'Emmett's just so good in bed I don't even think about it any more,' she says.

'Can I write that down?' I ask.

'Yeah, you can,' Nina says. 'I mean in Mangia [a text game she made] there's a whole part where I talk about having sex with him. When you get to a certain part it says, "Do you want to have sex with Emmett now?" And you can. And it just talks about how I feel after sex. His co-workers played it and were horrified.

'I've liked having sex for different reasons. Now I like it because it feels like the only time I'm not stressed about anything.'

'Yes. Yes,' I say. 'Yes.'

'And you can just ignore everything.'

'And pay attention to just one person you care about,' I say. 'I'm not sure I've had a one-night stand where I didn't care about the other person. When I was in Paris, Katharine told me that the French don't really use the word for love like we would, and so the English–French translation can be awkward. It's almost like everything is on a spectrum of love for them, I think she was telling me. I started to think about how I previously considered love a binary state, but I agree that it's more like a spectrum from barely giving a shit about the other person to really giving a shit about them.'

'It shouldn't be a logic problem: "If I am in love with X,

then I can have sex with them",' Nina says. 'It's never like that. There are so many reasons people have sex. That needs to be culturally acceptable. With Emmett I can just stop being stressed. Feel normal for a while. Which is funny – "I only feel normal when I have sex" – but that's so true. Because otherwise I feel so self-conscious with people, with jobs, with objects, that I can never feel natural.'

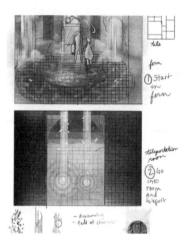

'With poetry I hit a wall,' Nina tells me. 'And I got really sick, and I started making games, and I realised games were another way that I could express myself and feel that kind of agency again. Agency in that I knew I could make things that could attract people to me. Because I just like people. And I want them to engage with my work.

'Hopefully I can get them to engage in a meaningful way,' she says. 'Engage with the issues that I faced growing up. I still have a lot of baggage from being a kid that I just haven't gotten to explore. The most rewarding way for me to explore that is unfortunately by having other people to talk with me about it or having the awareness that other people are engaging with it. Because then I am getting this sense of not being totally alone. My parents made me feel alone by brushing off everything that I was doing. Seeing people interact with the things I make, actually play it, feels like they are actively engaged with what I am trying to say.'

'I feel the same way about my work,' I say. 'When I write anything. The power of self-mythologising – it gives me a sense of control over my life. And I also feel less alone when people identify with something that happened to me. I feel power. I feel control when I do not feel in control of anything else in my life.'

'Yes,' Nina says. 'And also I might have said this the other night – it gives me a sense of validation. I never really got validation from my family, and you never really got it from school because it feels so artificial because you are paying to go there. But when people play your games and actually express something about it, whether that's feedback or a facial recognition that they'd finished it, you can see that they recognise that's an experience that you can express through a game. Or at least I can pretend that's what they're thinking and it makes me feel better about myself.'

'Girls are always told that they're crazy, or that their emotions aren't real,' Nina says. 'They'll be like, "Oh, you're just saying that", or whatever. People have always said that to me. I feel like maybe games are like, "No. Fuck you. I'm not crazy. *This shit is real.*"'

'I think part of the power of autobiographical games – or even when I write something very personal – is in forcing someone to identify with you,' I say to Nina, picking at tempura. 'Limiting their available options. Forcing someone into that tiny vignette space. It's very powerful. The idea that someone might feel the same way if they experience the same things is so powerful.'

'There's a lot of hope putting something out in the world that someone will come back to you,' Nina says. 'With How Do You Do It, I had a lot of people, men and women, coming back to me saying, "I did that exact same thing." It made me feel really good about myself. And Ladylike to a lesser extent.'

New York runs Streets of Rage on a janky framework
And in tunnels
The rat AI is broken

Environment art from Cibele

Cibele is being made via a series of game jams, as Nina
works full-time at Kickstarter as an intern. She is making
the game as designer, programmer, producer and actor for
the cut scenes. Emmett Butler, her boyfriend, is helping with
additional programming. Decky Coss is the composer, sound
designer and audio engineer. Rebekka Dunlap is making the
art, and Samantha Corey, Nina's flatmate, is the filmmaker
filming the cut scenes. Justin Briner is voice acting.

Cibele is still being made, but the MMOesque sections,
built to simulate Nina's experiences playing with a guy who
flirted with her via voicechat while playing, are already striking
with placeholder art. The act of playing those sections of the
game – killing monsters, some seeming symbolic of Nina's
emotional state – while people have an awkwardly intimate
conversation over the play, seems dramatic and engaging.
Every time the player goes to kill a monster, the overbearing
male AI player kills it first.

'I have this personality where I just let people walk all
over me,' Nina says. 'Whenever I talk to people about Cibele
I say, "Oh, I know, it's such a selfish thing to try and make a
game about," but ultimately I'm making it for a lot of reasons,

a large one of them because it's cathartic and I still have issues with this whole scenario. It was pretty scarring for me. But also I've heard so many other people who have been through similar situations.

'It's really a stigmatised scenario where you meet someone in a game and then you have sex with them or have a relationship with them. It's a taboo to even talk about it. The only way I'll be able to get over it is talking really loudly about it, so we can't ignore it any more. No matter what the reaction is, I'll automatically feel better about it. That's why I'm super dedicated to being super honest about it. That's why I want to have the sex scene, have people be nude. It's like Allen Ginsberg and the Beat Poets: he would talk about giving people blow jobs in a graphic way. A lot of people hated him for that. But that's honesty. He did do that. So you have to be able to write about that.'

I nod in agreement. 'All my most popular work on the internet has been when I have been most honest about something that no one else wanted to be honest about. I even opened one of these with "I woke up on a chiptune artist".'

'Same,' Nina says, and giggles. 'That's the perfect thing to make art about. It's the sort of thing that people who aren't as confident, or don't have the self-esteem to talk about it publicly, will be so thankful to see. Not only do you get to fulfil this selfish desire for validation but other people get to feed off that validation by being like, "Whoa, I'm not this person who did this terrible thing". Especially when it's sex. Women having casual sex. There's so much shame and guilt. Especially when you make games about sex.'

Screenshot from Cibele

'Why is sex with Emmett so good?'

'I think it's because we're so good at communicating. Ever since we started dating we never had an issue telling each other what we want. Or what scares us, which is even more important. When we first started having sex I'd just gotten out of a relationship with a guy who was sort of abusive and who was a mutual friend of ours. So there was this tension from the beginning that this was definitely not allowed, even though that's not true – that's a cultural expectation, that you can't sleep with someone after a certain amount of time after you've had a breakup. So our first challenge was to talk to each other and say, "Are we comfortable having sex?" And after talking we found out we were. But I feel like that set an expectation. Talking was really important, especially when it came to sex.'

'Do you talk during sex?'

'Yes. Not necessarily during, but before and after. And if I want to do something different I just ask.'

'Do you appraise afterwards?'

'Oh yeah. Literally every time we're done we're like, "That was so good" or "That was okay". Or if one of us is feeling like the other is being a little disingenuous about it ... it helps just to be asked and forced to be like, "Yeah, I'm feeling kind of out of it". But that obviously took a long time to learn. We're good at it now. Which is why we have such good sex.'

'I've had pretty amazing sex without ever having to say a word to the other person,' I say.

'But it could be so much better!' Nina says, and she's right.

I say, 'Once this one guy was like, "I want you to get on top", and before that I didn't usually because I find it hard to have a good time on top for one reason or another – or maybe it's that I didn't find the right partner with the right body shape, or maybe I'm wired differently. I feel a lot like in bed I'm naturally submissive, I like to be thrown around a little, which is something people don't automatically think about me – y'know, dom in the streets, sub in the sheets. Anyway, I got on top and he taught me to like it. It was like I had an orgasm coach. It was pretty great to make him happy and get something out of it. And I told him, and he was like, "Uh, well, I just thought it was always easier for women on top", which I guess is an assumption he'd made. Or maybe it was an excuse he was making to excuse his selfishness in that regard.'

'I always hated on top too, but my reasons were that I was so self-conscious about my body. I'd always feel gross and fat about being on top. But Emmett likes it. And now I like it. Because I see him liking it, which makes me feel actually good about myself.'

Character art, Cibele

'When I was making How Do You Do It I wanted it to be humorous,' Nina explains. 'I feel like childhood sexuality is something that we're taught to be ashamed of. I think that's bullshit. Cibele is not humorous, but I think there's a time and a place for addressing sex in games and media. There's a time to be really serious about it too, and be like, people are affected by this.

'But especially when you're trying to convey conversations between real people. We use humour in our daily conversations always,' she continues. 'That's just something that we do. It's part of our culture. And I was writing Cibele based on conversations that I remember happening. It's interesting to see how the humour manifests itself both in regular humour but also in some of the situations where it's more like ironic humour, or you know where this is going. "Look, he's saying this flirtatious thing." It's not that it's funny, but you laugh at it because he's trying to get in her pants. I'm seeing humour come out in that way in the game. Also when people are super bigoted it's kind of hilarious. There are parts in it where the guy is just the worst. You're sort of laughing at that because it is so awful. And that's more like dark humour.'

'How about looking a person in the eyes?' I ask. 'I find it difficult to do that in bed unless I know that it isn't just something throwaway. Or sometimes that's my indication that it isn't just nothing, the ability to be able to hold a gaze.'

'Even with Emmett I don't usually look him right in the eyes,' Nina says. 'I usually do it once, but I can never do it the whole time. I feel like it's almost too intense. I'm sure there'll be a day where I want that intensity and we'll do it the whole time. But usually ... yeah, there's something about it. Because sex has that effect where you are not worrying about other things, you become super vulnerable. There's something super intense about looking at someone while you're both vulnerable, that's really ... frightening. It's easier to do with someone you love because you are vulnerable with each other all the time. Being in love with someone is basically being vulnerable with someone all the time. But for me it's too high-risk to exchange that vulnerability with someone I am not committed to. But I feel like I can give a little bit of that away with Emmett, who I am in love with, and who I am committed to.'

'I feel a lot like I am vulnerable all the time,' I say.

'Which is why I get hurt all the time.'

*

I look down the carriage
People look away but
A small grey-haired lady looks up at me
'Do you need this seat?' she says.
'Not at all.'
'AGE BEFORE BEAUTY!' another old lady exclaims
Sitting.
'You are very beautiful,' the first old lady says, Jersey accent.
'I like your purple hair,' she says.
The train leaves
And my heart calms.
It is the city of aggressive love
People are fire humans here

'The major issue is that it makes it impossible to forget,' Nina says. 'You can forget things that happen while your eyes are closed. There's something about seeing someone … I don't know what it is. Communication with the eyes. But there's something about that – you get a feeling and you just can't forget it. It's just there now. Filed away in your memory.'

'Maybe we need more eyes-open sex in games,' I say. 'In terms of designers being vulnerable. Taking risks. Getting hurt.'

'Yeah, that's why we have so many Mario clones. Risk averse.'

Boring sex.

Nina tells me about a set of vignettes by one author she once played. She said of all the little vignettes, there was only one that rang true as a personal narrative: it was about a painful breakup.

'This,' Nina says, pointing at the invisible creator of the breakup game, 'THIS is the game that you WANTED to make. Whoever made this game went through an awful breakup and wanted to make a game about it – but then felt like they had to pad it with all these other games just to make it more like a "game". You can see that the personal story shines.'

in any case, i think i'll
trespass the café
where everyone is beautiful and
changing the world with a single
earth shattering click
because i want to
be cool too

i wear crop tops to
professional events and
listen to rave music at Staples
hi-chew for breakfast
sega dreamcast catcher
wake up and
smell the
neighbors smoking
cloves

'this view is extraordinary'
i sigh and
stare deeply

into the horizon of my
macbook desktop,
the sun slowly uploading
into day

From <u>Untitled</u> by Nina Freeman

I am in New York, freshly off the plane from Los Angeles and everyone talks about the Barcades, bars where there are arcade cabinets. I meet Nina at Barcade in Brooklyn where she knows a barman, and we talk about scripting and feelings and scripting feelings. Later I get off the 6 at 86th Street alone and walk out onto the sidewalk and it begins to rain. It rains hard, and no one is on the streets but me.

When it rains hard in Manhattan it is Fuck Buttons' Brainfreeze.

The rain pelts down and the streets are BBC Micro black. The street lights cast faint white highlights, Elite style, on tall Gotham structures. The brown subway soup that my flip-flops have scooped into my toes is flushed out into the huge invisible puddles of broad Manhattan streets. I stop by the light of a shop window to be engulfed.

I remember showing my ID to the bouncer at the Barcade entrance and smile. The tarmac is being hammered; I am sure it will crack.

I spit water from my lips. People are making out hard in Manhattan speakeasies. They are making out to show other people. They are making out because there isn't enough time. They are making out for everyone. It is raining out here.

I showed my ID at the Barcade entrance. I know I am ready to be old. We are ready to be old.

Let's be old together.

Embed with ...
Adriaan de Jongh

I was incredibly sick this month and everything was beset with disasters. This piece is a little shorter, but it's about Game Oven's Adriaan de Jongh, designer of games Fingle, Friendstrap and Bounden.

Prologue: Beyond the Sea

It's all fun and games until you get sick.

Rewind to the journey before: dazed on a platform at Gatwick airport, England, the train has broken down, rubbing eyes coffee-wired, sleep sucked down greedy but not enough to soothe the sting of leaving New York's lazy fluorescence, barking demeanour, franks and knishes, intrusions, flounces, laughs. The last late embraces in the cool grass under a flat sun. Elizabeth in shorts, knees up on a cast-iron garden chair and a beer labelled 'Raging Bitch', Nina on a barstool at Barcade grinning, pink Botticelli hair and freckles. She wondered then: what will be written? It was written, Khaleesi.

I stand on the platform and cry to Siouxsie and the Banshees. I hope some mascara is running down my face for Cities In Dust's sake. I try to save my emotions for when I am alone, because it might be rude to be overwhelmed in someone else's company.

Days later Bowie's 'Let's Dance' comes on in the coffee shop where I sit: three of the Old Guard flail their arms over laptops and sing about trembling like a flower loud over my complaints about game criticism, the economics of writing. They warble about serious moonlight and they all laugh. *Cara, this is a microcosm of your problems, the Old Guard singing over your troubles!*

And I laugh because, yes, it is, and, well, it's funny. It's funny. It feels good to laugh. It feels right, in a way, that they have security, and I am writing from my lap in parks and bedsits and outside under dripping air-conditioning units being bitten alive, because they seem so certain of who they are, and I am some sort of poltergeist trying to break through the windows of the internet, stuck in a weird limbo between employed and unemployed, exploited and exploiting, out of the loop and so deep in the loop I want to run away. Perhaps someday someone will find me when I'm the hot messy heart of the internet, hyperventilating like a bird in a cat's mouth, jagged with shards of games and bleeding into some sort of word gutter with a manic grin on my face, a grin of triumph, a euphoric cackle emanating from six thousand drunk arcade-adjacent selfies.

Nine Worlds convention comes and goes; I stay away from most of it to be alone. I have a bath for the first time in two months in the hotel room, the hook of my arm slumped over the lip of it while *The Thick of It* yelps from the laptop, drawing sharp black ink clouds over London though it is sunny outside. Heavy-handled cutlery in palms over dinner at the Marriott, KG looks darkly at me as if the doubt has coloured my expression; we steal the bottle of red wine and talk about creation creeping in, lighting our evening cigarettes out in the wasteland of Heathrow, the furze bushes and the planes in the sky flaring into fire. When I leave I do not say goodbye. I no longer need to.

Howard greets me at Ryde Harbour, I make him a game from his wispy grey illustrations, illustrations that have me drift into daydreams, I write Yannick in New York an email from the couch at midnight and as soon as I arrive I have left, the hovercraft drifting in the wind like Desert Bus over the road.

Amsterdam

The person I was going to cover this month had to leave their home suddenly, meaning I cannot visit. It's the last two weeks of August and I'm desperate. Three people can help me: Aureia Harvey in Belgium, Mitu Khandaker in England and Rami Ismail in The Netherlands. Aureia is busy but recommends Pietro Righi Riva in Verona; Pietro is busy. Mitu is on holiday. Rami is leaving, but he suggests Adriaan de Jongh.

Adriaan is free. I buy the cheapest one-way flight from London into Amsterdam Schipol at 6 a.m.

Adriaan comes to arrivals late – big hair, tall, smiling, and with more energy than my body knows it can deal with. 'Hello!' he says, warmly, and we hug. He insists on looping my heavy bag over his shoulder and saunters off to get me a transit card. Adriaan de Jongh is the designer-programmer of the games Fingle, Friendstrap and Bounden, among other things. He worked on these games with his Game Oven co-founder, developer Bojan Endrovski. The most recent addition to the Game Oven team is Eline Muijres, who is on board to help with marketing. Game Oven's games are a genre unto their own: they are a hybrid of videogames and board games built on provoking players to use the play space outside their screen.

Adriaan lives in Amsterdam and commutes to Game Oven's office in Utrecht, forty minutes away by train. Utrecht is home to the Dutch Game Garden, a large modern complex full of The Netherlands' most talented game people.

Later in the Game Oven office I'd see a sign, FINGLE

GOT ME LAID, pinned to a wall haphazardly: asking Adriaan about it, he'd tell me stories of all the people who had played Fingle together and embarked on romantic relationships with each other.

The most 'famous' of these romantic couples, he tells me, is the developer Adriel Wallick and Vlambeer Games' Rami Ismail. 'Rami met Adriel and played Fingle for three hours on the plane,' Adriaan says. They are now travelling the world with each other.

How it works is this: you download the game to your iPad and get a partner. It's a good idea to check that this partner knows that they are going to have to touch your fingers when you play this game: you are going to get close. Then you begin the first level: place fingers on the little squares. Some squares are white, some are yellow, denoting each player's fingers. Your job is to move those squares into place inside empty dotted-line squares.

This usually requires your hands rubbing another player's hands rhythmically as the empty squares move. It's like Twister for the hands, but this time it is accompanied by the sound of a guitar with a wah-wah pedal, and when you complete a level it rewards you with a deep voice sighing phrases like 'ooh yeaaaaaah'.

'Someone told me a story,' Adriaan says to me. 'This girl ... she had a boyfriend at the time, and then she Fingled with someone else ... and that became a thing. There's lots of stories like that.'

I tell Adriaan Fingle once made me very uncomfortable, because it required me to be physically close to someone else at a party when I wasn't ready. I told Adriaan it made me think harder about intimacy, about how Fingle requires you not only to physically touch another person's hands, but that it requires you to both have the same will to complete a task together. You both have to want to do something. It's almost a game about consent. About permission for closeness.

Fingle might have silly overtones, but it didn't stop me leaving my proposed partner sitting alone, the task incomplete, while I went to find a stiffer drink.

'That's the reason I make games,' Adriaan says to me. 'What Fingle can address is the relationship between you and the other person. And do things to it.'

All of Adriaan's designs are about the game outside of the game.

*

I walk out of Schipol airport trailing Adriaan. Somewhere in the back of my mind I know I am sick, though the usual symptoms are not yet showing.

I have been eating diner food on no sleep for weeks. Everything is tiring. When I am tired like this I look up at the sky a lot, can't focus on people's eyes; their focus on me becomes tiring. I feel like Marty McFly's family in his photograph as we make our way via tram through the beautiful streets of Amsterdam, walking past demure red brick buildings with delicate green leaves rambling up the sides, arched doorways with triangle roofs and little square balconies. Adriaan lives a few streets away from the van Gogh museum in a tiny studio apartment. He says he managed to move into the most expensive area of Amsterdam because his mother used to live in this exact same room when she was at university here, and knows the landlady.

Adriaan's suggestion for our first night: a party, then a club. These two things are my favourite things. Of course I say yes. Of course.

Delirium

Hours later we arrive at a club that I cannot remember the name of. We are on the guest list; Adriaan knows the DJ because he sometimes makes music for games. The club is small and dark with the usual neon lights. Strips of white light are affixed to the walls, the bar glows blue. Trent Kusters and

Blake Mizzi from the game Armello are in Amsterdam, and they are joining me, Eline and Adriaan, and we disperse to dance.

It is the sort of club where people arrive with Intentions.

'There's no game that comes close to this,' Adriaan says, next to me.

I nod. 'Fingle is the only game that comes even close,' I say. 'And that's still pretty far away.'

I feel delirious, like the lights are bleaching my brain; drowsy. I ask Blake for Red Bull, and then another Red Bull, and my weariness is still not shaking off. There's a girl dancing on the stage in hot pants. I want to be here. But I am not.

My fevered brain realises the fashion in here is to have very long undyed hair. I am a tall woman with short purple hair now. Men keep trying to talk to me and I just can't give them my attention. A man wearing a T-shirt advertising an app company tries to talk to me and just won't leave me alone. *I'm a journalist and here's your review: Cara throws up on your feet.*

Do you go to a club to talk?

Do you go to a brothel to talk?

The whole club seems too slow; there's a techno DJ on but I can't find anything in the music to hook dancing to. Next to me Trent is talking to a tall hot girl, and I realise they have been talking, not dancing, for hours. I have developed an incredible headache and my throat feels like it is on fire.

Can we surmise that Trent isn't coming home with us? I start to think, realising that I need to go home very badly. 'I think I'm coming down with something,' I say to Eline, who looks concerned. 'I guess I'll take some drugs and it'll be fine.' She looks appalled; my deadened brain understands that she has taken this to mean something like MDMA, not the ibuprofen I was daydreaming of.

Well, I remember thinking, that'd do. At least I wouldn't feel like this.

I don't remember the two days after that clearly, I don't even remember if Trent did come home, but I do remember lying on the mattress in Adriaan's room and hallucinating, in pain, overheating, unable to breathe, never aware when Adriaan was there or not, listening to Drake albums and having the sort of suffocating sinus pain where you think your face is just attached to a giant headcrab. My temperature seemed so high sometimes I kept thinking people were lying next to me on the bed, but I'd move and they weren't. One night I had a dream that Drake was spooning my sweating body and whispering puns on the word 'ill' in my ear, telling me I am 'ill', though this sort of dream hasn't happened since I have recovered.

Which is just my fucking luck.

*

I come to on the mattress one morning and Adriaan throws cherry tomatoes at me from the kitchen. I laugh, and know I am better.

Prototyping

Learning to programme almost ruined Adriaan's life. He learned how to programme five years ago, and did nothing else for eight weeks straight, and it gave him severe health problems.

'It was really terrifying. But I've never been as productive in my life ever,' he tells me in the pub. 'How I got out of that is just not cool. I had troubles with breathing. I had to relearn how to breathe.

'I'd been a super energetic guy for most of my life. I've done most of the sports you know. From horse riding to soccer to tennis to baseball ... I've always had a lot of energy. Doing the programming non-stop, me sitting behind the computer was devastating for me. It sucked everything out of me.

'It's called chronic hyperventilation. You only exhale half of the carbon monoxide, which is weird. You think you're breathing normally but you're not. The veins in your brain sometimes contract, and it gives you a very scary feeling. It feels like you are suffocating ... I really had to relearn breathing.'

'Is that why you mainly make games to do with physical movement?' I ask. The latest Game Oven project was Bounden, a game developed with the Dutch National Ballet, where two people hold on to a mobile device and move it together using their bodies to have a symbol move along a track.

'No, that's not the reason why,' he says.

I slump in my chair.

'I studied game design and development at the Utrecht School of the Arts,' Adriaan begins.

'How old are you?' I ask.

'I'm twenty-three,' he says.

Ugh.

'I didn't learn anything about making games at HKU for the first two years,' Adriaan says. 'I did not make a game until the second half of my first third year. But fortunately the first half of my third year I did my internship at Vanguard, which made Gatling Gears, and are now working on the Halo franchise. There are fifty people there. They had a design document in the form of a Wikipedia there. And all the designers, six, seven people were working on that, typing documents all day long ... But this one guy, he would also work on it for a couple of weeks, but at some point he started coming to work with prototypes.

'So he'd come to work in the morning and he'd be like, "Hey, Adriaan, check out this prototype I made last night. It's a networked multiplayer game." It blew my mind. He did that in an evening. So that inspired me.'

'Well,' I say, 'I thought designers make prototypes. That

makes a lot of sense to me.'

'To me it does,' Adriaan says. 'But not to everyone. If you look at The Netherlands and the people who call themselves game designers, at least fifty per cent cannot write a single line of code.'

'What was the first thing you made?'

'I bought an Apple developer licence. My dad bought an iPad and said, "Oh, you wanna make games? Make games for this." I said, "I'm gonna do that." The first thing I made was a game where you drag a giraffe neck up and down and you had to avoid birds hitting its face. A super silly game, but that was the start of my game design career. From that point on,' Adriaan says, 'I made a lot of shit.'

But he didn't make shit forever. Fingle went on to be a finalist for an IGF award. Bounden was funded so that Game Oven could work with the Dutch National Ballet on a game about movement. Even Friendstrap is a very elegantly designed conversation machine.

All you do is load it up on a phone and find a partner you would like to get to know better. It will give you an awkward or unusual conversation topic, and you have to discuss it for just under ten minutes. You do it while pressing your thumb onto the screen with the other person, attaching you to each other in a subtle manner. You get lost in the conversation, until the phone vibrates, and you have to release your fingers and press again for another topic.

It's such a simple idea, but I played it with Eline at a party and it worked so well that I felt almost annoyed that no one had made it before. It felt very natural. Much less awkward than trying to talk about the weather. The more absurd topics of conversation in Friendstrap may include:

Eye contact

Making sound effects

Licking your elbow

Silent farting

Sex in space
Muffin top
Invisible hands
Sing a song

Why is it that Adriaan designs the games he does? They are so different from what I always thought of games being. They are about moving and togetherness. They are about being close to someone. They are about changing the relationship you have with another person.

I think it is partly to do with the realisation that he didn't have to make the games that everyone else was making. That he could strike out on his own.

'The project I did in my third year,' he says, 'after my internship, was a game to rehabilitate people with hemiplegia.

'Half their motor functions are impaired. You can regain the core motor functions by doing a lot of exercising. The idea was to make a game to help those people rehabilitate, to make it more fun. I was in a team with a lot of guys who didn't really want to make this game. They wanted to make shooters. You know, the fans, the gamers. And now they have to make a rehabilitation game and everyone's like, oh fuck this. But I took the project super seriously, we made it through, and we won Dutch game awards.'

Real Life

We sit on the grass in the Vondelpark, forty-seven hectares of green landscaping with ponds and streams, and ducks that quietly quack at the constant passing of bicycles. We make cornbread sandwiches and Adriaan laments the lack of imagination in mainstream games. I think what he is talking about is a divide between commerce and art, or at least the conflict between what art wants and what the market wants and how the artist technically needs to serve both to survive.

'One day I'd like the reason we make games to be the '

same as the reasons people make art,' Adriaan says.

I think about this for a while: it's funny, because it might not appear to be that way right now, but I think there are a wealth of people out there doing that. Adriaan is one of them.

His outlook is incredibly hardline: he is headstrong. He sometimes absolutely cannot see why anyone would not want to do something the way that he does it; he is very blunt and direct. I think he is the same way as a designer: he gave a talk at GDCE emphasising how there should be absolutely no compromise towards the designer's 'vision' for what the game should be and do. It has certainly led to games that are, in themselves, directly what he wanted. He wanted to provoke relationships between players.

Most of all, it's comforting to see someone be so goddamn certain about the future, and their place in it.

*

'This ending seems very abrupt,' Adriaan says to me. 'You finish on the beginning of my career.'

This month is terrible, I think. I am not myself. I am broken. I can't do endings. LEAVE ME ALONE, ADRIAAN. I pour another glass of wine and cough into it.

'What do you want to make in the future?' I ask him.

'I will make things that are very different from what you know me for,' he says. 'I am looking for the mechanics that fit my vision. That's the Holy Grail of game design.'

'That seems very vague,' I say. For you, the readership.

'Well, it is vague,' he says. 'But I think especially the vision is vague. I mean, I know what I mean about mechanics. And you probably know what I mean about mechanics. But the vision is gonna happen to me. It just has to be organic.'

'What platform will your most amazing game be on?' I ask, grinning.

'This is going to sound really cheesy,' he says.

'Say it.'

'REAL LIFE,' Adriaan says. He smiles.

We laugh pretty hard at this.

'In the end any game happens in your mind. Even for this stupid device.' He picks up an iPhone. 'It all happens in your mind. That fact – that's going to help remind me of what it's all about.'

Embed with ...
Shawn Beck

Shawn with Keiji Inafune

This month I embedded in Malaysia with the developer Shawn Beck, maker of the newly released Velocibox.

LOADING ...

There used to be a cheat code for Tomb Raider II – a complicated series of steps where you lit a flare and danced, the screen would go black and the CD would rev in the drive. A step forward? A step back? A jump, maybe.

Each flight I take is like a rev in the drive. I sleep and wake up and everything is different. The requirements are different, the objectives unknown, new environments wait.

I think about how cheat coded I feel by planes as the palm trees fly by; twelve hours of mascara stings my eyes and I smell of KLM green tea handwash. Kuala Lumpur's hot damp clings and shimmers. The cheat code has kicked me across time and space. It kicks like a son of a bitch. It kicks brutal in the gut. It keeps happening.

'Most people in KL will greet you with "Have you eaten?"' my friend and Rock Paper Shotgun colleague Cassandra

Khaw shouts from the front seat as her mother guns it down the wide flat asphalt. This month's fixer, Cass, is teaching me about Kuala Lumpur food culture.

People have a similar greeting in Edinburgh. We do a demure-sounding 'You'll have had your tea?' which, particularly coming from older people, is a preamble to stuffing you with scones or steak pie. I'm skinny from being ill last month, and this month I will learn that Cass is the equivalent of an Edinburgh grandmother. I will trail her around malls being refilled like a Pez dispenser, only instead of candy it is hot butter Rotiboys, satay, savoury pastries, roti bon, Thai food, every kind of curry.

Cass instructs me on the city:

Wear a bra
Don't go out after twelve
Boil the water before drinking it
Don't leave your phone on the table
Don't barter while white ('you are very white')
Don't eat where there are roaches (disobeyed)
Don't get ripped off (failed – twice)

Cass warns me about the dickish taxi drivers. Once, she says, she went to archery practice and afterwards fell asleep in the back of a taxi. The driver realised she was asleep and drove hours away from where Cass had asked to be dropped. When Cass woke and realised there could be a number of things that might be happening to her hours away from home, she slowly drew an arrow from her bag and pressed the point of it into the driver's neck. She held it there for hours until she was at her front door.

I promise myself only to get into taxis highly caffeinated.

Thick stretches of palm trees line the roads, huge concrete-buffered roads wider than I have ever seen, even in LA. The skies are bigger and mistier here, and my slow brain thinks

hm
hm
hm
hm

To the music of the road, Cass explains that everyone speaks more than one language, describes the diverse ethnic mix of Kuala Lumpur, and tells me how easy it is to insult people by not reading their race and cultural background. I nod and try to breathe everything in, noting that I can at least recognise spoken Cantonese if not Malay. Cars around us brake abruptly; motorbikes weave in and out of them like mechanical deer.

I look at my battered UK passport. Back in Scotland, there will be a vote this month on whether or not I will still be British. Malaysia escaped the British a while back, and although it isn't the same situation by any stretch, Scotland always had a chip on its shoulder about being 'colonised'. I'm not sure how I feel about any of it. I want the people who still live there to make the decision.

The undulating palm leaves and spiked bushes go by in a muggy haze; it is monsoon season.

That cheat code for Tomb Raider II – a system of steps and jumps. Deftly completed, it would throw you forward into the next level. It was like waking to a new place each time: emerald valleys, Venice canals, rocky overtures with promise of secrets, medipacks stuck in caverns as chocolate chips in a dense cake. I would try to take nothing from the levels, jumping to the next when it became apparent I couldn't proceed without stealing.

The waking was the thing. A fade in, and you raise her head to see where you might go.

At some point, you'd wake underwater, and, unable to do the cheat 'dance' at the bottom of the ocean, you had to survive until you found an air pocket and a place to orientate yourself.

Cassandra finally provides me with one: she puts me in a tiny studio apartment in Neo Damansara, overlooking a giant mall called The Curve. It has a small gym in the building, and a pool.

For some of this month I sleep in a room alone. There is a washing machine in the apartment. There's air conditioning. It is quiet but for the rush of the water by my window into the pool below my floor. When I lie by the pool reading, swallows fly from above, dipping and skimming across the water to drink, and then out, wheeling into the dappled grey-blue sky. Food nearby is ridiculously cheap: two ringgit for lunch, and Cass informs me this is expensive.

Being alone in this apartment is a kind of therapy. I listen a lot to Jessie Ware's 'Tough Love' because it is like listening to the beat of my own heart.

I am so thankful for this room. I play The Sims 4 when I need company, and drink cold water looking over the sunset. When I leave in a dazed, relaxed state from this month, I send a huge bouquet of flowers to Cass with a fuzzy teddy bear to say thank you, because I think psychological peace like that might only happen again when I finish writing this series for good.

Breakfast near the IGN Asia offices. I meet some of the IGN team, among them Max Villandre, a Canadian who is now creative director for IGN Asia, but who moved here twelve years ago, a veteran animator. When he arrived, universities and colleges were teaching Flash. Max had a different idea: C# to open games studios. It took him four to five years' work with the Malaysian government to get developers who knew how to programme for big-budget games. He opened Codemasters Malaysia with the newest talent.

'I've been here for twelve years. I've been working hard, I can tell you that!' He laughs as we sit over beer. 'I've worked with governments here and in Singapore because they understood they needed these structures.'

A perfectionist, Max directed the team that was nominated for a BAFTA for Colin McRae: Dirt 2. The game perfectly recreates some beautiful Malaysian landscapes. 'We were really proud of that Malaysian track,' Max says. 'That was probably one of the best things [Codemasters Malaysia] have done.'

*

Have I mentioned before that I love roads, and driving games? And I love roads in driving games. I think it is half because I can't drive, half because I like the therapy of it, the journey and not the climax. But now as I sit here in a Tokyo armchair remembering Kuala Lumpur, all I can think of is that first drive Cass's mother navigated from the airport, and all I can do is look at this video of Max's game with the sound off.

Of course, Kuala Lumpur is a built-up concrete-and-glass city and there are no dirt tracks. The road from the airport is a huge motorway of the wide, long, flat asphalt kind. But the road is lined with those trees. Staring at the lush trees and plants in Dirt 2 is enough to evoke the feeling of being there. I feel like I am in a thick, delicious-smelling cloud of Malaysian foodstuffs when I look at it. I feel like I am floating through the car-clogged streets of the city, following my nose into cafés and restaurants full of the kind of food you only taste when you're asleep, because your imagination makes it up.

*

Awaiting butter crab

Kuala Lumpur has a small games development community, and this is an awkward time. September is Tokyo Game Show month, and everyone is preparing for it. Max takes me out for dinner and a pint of KL Guinness before becoming too busy with work to meet again. Cass takes me to a late-night mamak to meet Bazil Akmal Bidin, the head of the Malaysian International Game Developers Association, and while we chat amiably Cass stuffs me with more roti as I am bitten alive by mosquitoes that only seem to favour Scottish flesh.

It's here that Bazil introduces me to <u>Shawn Beck</u>.

Shawn was born and raised in Kuala Lumpur. He released his twitch-heavy action game <u>Velocibox</u> on Steam just after I arrived in Malaysia. It was only his second solo game, if you discount a Ludum Dare browser game called Pew Pew Pew Pew, and Shawn seems sort of reluctant to talk about the game before it.

Velocibox

So far Velocibox has received very high ratings on Steam, but very few journalists have covered it. It's something in the vein of Super Hexagon, a knowing homage, but it's very much its own thing – I've seen it before but I'm disastrous at twitch games. I'm the worst at Super Hexagon. I prefer to watch ex-*Edge* editor Jason Killingsworth and the game creator himself, Terry Cavanagh, face off at high scores on Super Hexagon, mesmerising with the shapes and entrancing me with the Chipzel soundtrack, rather than ever attempt to get good at it. When I mention that I know Terry Cavanagh, and that he punched a birthday cake in front of me, Shawn's eyes brighten and he suddenly becomes very talkative.

Community is a wonderful thing.

Later, Cass asks Shawn if he'll give me a lift home in his car. We're pretty far away from where I live, and Cass' taxi anecdotes have been somewhat daunting.

'We know where you live if she doesn't come back,' Cass tells Shawn, possibly more darkly than she meant.

As we walk to Shawn's car, we get to talking a bit about Shawn's background. He's had a similar childhood to me, limited access to consoles, a bit of PC gaming, struggles with parents to let him buy games. As a grown-up he eventually got a job working for Autodesk on Maya, the graphics software package, and left when he knew he had something to make. But he'd always loved games, always wanted to make them.

I think I realised I'd like to write about Shawn when I asked him about the first game he ever loved, and he said Day Of The Tentacle. We talked about its weirdness, its humour, our fascination with its intricate parts, in the car ride home on the huge long roads of KL, flashes of white light illuminating the tall buildings, malls flying by with gaudy signs.

Day Of The Tentacle

Shawn says he loved the Chron-O-John in Day Of The Tentacle most of all, and we become a little bit quiet and sentimental thinking about those Lost Days, the days when adventure game interfaces were frictionless because they were necessary. Now, those cursed instructional interfaces are the scourge of the ScummVM engine, using it is clumsy, like a set of tall, heavy-based traffic cones sitting between you and your long-lost love's embrace, or like a greased ball pool pit between you and the last slice of cake. But the memories preserve the pleasure for you. You don't have to do anything to enjoy Day Of The Tentacle any more; you just select the record and play the animations in your head.

I ask Shawn if he ever wanted to make adventure games, but he tells me he swore off making story-based games. He says he isn't any good at stories, and I understand, knowing that I am only good at stories.

*

One night, I need good internet to file my Rock Paper Shotgun column, and Cass sneaks me in to use the wifi at the top of her luxury condo building (good wifi is hard to find here in KL). The 'Sky Lounge' looks over the city, the haze outside stretching up into the clouds.

*

Pyramid mall, KL

Cass's KL food culture stories have rubbed off on me, and so I ask Shawn if he'll take me to lunch one day.

He takes me to the best Nasi Lemak in Kuala Lumpur at the Village Park Restaurant. It is rammed full of people. The decor is basic – it's really just a small food hall where everything is very simple and they pack diners in. We hustle for a seat. I swear to God, when the food comes it is the most amazing thing I have ever put in my body. The fried chicken has a delicate, crispy skin that is just right, with juicy, melting chicken underneath. The fragrant coconut rice is some sort of fluffy magic. The chilli sauce is so sweet and moreish I want to scoop it direct into my mouth without putting it on anything.

I glance up at the picture on the wall: it's the family who run the restaurant smiling over all the diners.

'Typical Malaysian family,' Shawn says. The family members are all from different ethnic backgrounds: Malay, Chinese, Indian, and I think I even spy a stray European-looking man.

I remember Cass telling me that visual recognition of difference is important here, and wonder if that is the reason that people seem to respect each other so much, in their relaxed way – because they are educated in how differences between cultures should be accommodated and adapted to. There's no one 'culture' to be assimilated into like we try to do in the west, and as a result KL has none of the paranoid feel of a place bound by racial tensions like London is, even though it's a place where so many world cultures intersect.

We drink bubble tea beside a stuffed fox with antlers in a nearby shop. I distract myself enough to ask Shawn if it's hard to make games for a living in Malaysia.

'It's not hard to make games, it's just hard to make games that get attention,' he says. 'Here, there are only two companies who are doing just enough to survive a few months from one game. I'm mostly just doing one game at a time. I'm trying to do this thing solo. I've worked in a team before and it's just difficult trying to get your vision across. We have so many clashing ideas.'

'Most people I know have their full-time jobs and they're not able to give that up,' he continues. 'I mostly work with friends. I worked with a bunch of people one time, but the passion just wasn't there – because they were making the game based on monetisation plans. It wasn't about making the game fun, it was about when you persuade the players to pay money.

'I had a previous nine-to-five job that was paying me really well. I gave it up to make something that I really want. And if I'm doing that for someone else's vision, it defeats the purpose of going fully into game development.'

'Who do you make games for?' I ask.

'It's mostly for myself," Shawn says immediately. He smiles, then adds, 'BuZz [from the IGDA] tells me that's a weakness. He says, "Shawn can't make games for other people."'

I feel strangely touched by his certainty. A little flicker of my fourteen-year-old angsty little soul leaning over a 4 a.m. laptop keyboard, writing into a hard disk drive novels and short stories that will never see the light of day. They weren't meant for anyone else. But then, I wasn't doing it for a living. Shawn's commitment seems more admirable.

'That's how you continue,' Shawn says.

'But you must like people playing your games.'

'It's the best feeling in the world to watch people play and react to your game,' he says, and talks cheerfully of his Russian and Spanish Steam fans.

I ask Shawn about the economic viability of making games on your own. I ask if he'd ever stop making games if he suddenly found himself short on cash, but he says he wouldn't. Shawn goes on to tell me a story about Hafiz Azman, a student whose game Rhythm Doctor was nominated for the IGF this year. 'He worked on the game for three years, only during the summer. And he doesn't plan on going into development. And I think that's a good choice for him. He gets to keep a stable job as an engineer, and make games in his free time. And when you play Rhythm Doctor you can feel that passion oozing out, even though he's not an artist. That's the kind of game I admire.'

'Is a community important to you?'

'For me it's more the reassurance that you're going in the right direction,' Shawn says. 'Feedback is great, but for Velocibox I've learned that it's good not to listen to feedback sometimes. I actually had a conversation with someone on Twitter about why Velocibox has no checkpoints. So if you reach level seven and you die, you go back to level one.

'And a lot of people have opinions about this, saying, "You should have checkpoints." When I rolled the demo out I think everyone thought I'd make checkpoints for the final game. "Uuuuh, how am I supposed to tell them that isn't going to be in?" Even BuZz told me I should put in checkpoints. But deep down inside I knew I shouldn't. It just breaks the tension of the game.'

We have accidentally stumbled into a crucial conversation I often have with other critics and developers: whether critique is 'censorship' or is damaging in some way to developers. But it seems to Shawn that critique is actually very freeing: it illuminates the design choices he is making, it makes him consider how his game is constructed and what he intends the player to experience.

'Only you yourself know your game the best,' Shawn says.

It seems critique clarifies the choices, but you, the developer, call the shots.

*

The next day, Shawn flies out to show Velocibox at the Malaysia stand at the Tokyo Game Show, and I decide to follow him the day after and ask him more annoying questions about his experiences there. I do a drastic and hurried packing job on my only worldly possessions, I say a sad goodbye to the gym and the pool, because I have only just begun to feel the sinews in my body come alive again after months of having no idea if they were even there any more.

The taxi driver attempts to extract money from me on the way to the airport by suggesting we go the 'tourist route'. This has happened several times already; people tell me there are really no buildings in KL that are worth seeing apart from the Pyramid mall where everything is mocked up to look like it's Ancient Egyptian but is smothered in fairy lights and gold paint. (Seriously the most incredible mall I've ever been in.) I make the taxi driver go direct to the airport, making pointed glances at the telephone number on the taxi door that says to report drivers who overcharge. I know it's what Cass would want me to do.

I apologetically exchange dollars, ringgit, and pounds Sterling all into yen at a money exchange, making the clerk extremely grumpy.

I get into Tokyo Haneda just after midnight. The airport is deserted; my flight was delayed by two hours.

I feel strange here in the familiar surrounds of this airport. I try to shake it off. It's nothing, I think, and I tweet enthusiastically about having a party at Haneda airport, to which only the girl at the information desk is invited because no one else is here.

I try out my rusty Japanese on a young guy who is waiting at the taxi rank outside. We can share a cab ride to west Tokyo where I'm staying with my friend from Chicago, Jon. The guy's delighted – taxi fares are giant after midnight from Haneda and no trains are running. And we're both in Setagaya ku.

We chat in Japanese, dropping in English words as we go, mashing the languages together. I feel strange again, like the air is different here, like chatting with this young Japanese man in the back of a taxi is somehow being filmed for a TV show. I'm having this out-of-body experience where I look at myself from far away, only I am squinting.

I think I might be high or something. Am I running another fever? I didn't drink on the plane for once and I hardly had any caffeine.

*

The next few days are spent trailing past booths at the Tokyo Game Show, a place like any other game convention only the nerds are shorter and better-looking, most things are written in Japanese, and Solid Snake's Hideo Kojima comes out of his hutch to yell at crowds every so often. I idly think about pitching articles to publications, but I just can't bring myself to care about watching trailers or playing demos any more. I think I have given demos up forever. Just send me the whole game or I feel like a PR vehicle, or maybe more like a PR truck or those cars they have in *Jurassic Park*. Trailers and demos make me feel like a giant PR monster truck that you are trying to drive into a bunch of innocent bystanders via my loud, unfettered mouthpinions. Even when I do a preview of a game and hate it everyone shares it with each other and says, 'Look, Cara goofed off at this event', and then I've just become part of the marketing tactic all over again.

I find Shawn at his booth by the Malaysia stand, right by where he has to watch the new Metal Gear Solid trailer five times a day, and it seems he is getting some good feedback on his game, even if there's less foot traffic over here than by the Sony-sponsored indie stand, which is busy.

I catch up with him a day later, and we go to get my favourite meal, okonomiyaki, in Harajuku.

Shawn was sponsored to go to TGS. The Malaysian government offered to sponsor two teams to represent them at the Tokyo Game Show, which shows a commitment to developing a games industry, along with grants they make available to developers. The problem is that artists and designers can make more money in advertising, and programmers can make more money in apps, so tempting them away to make games is a hard slog. This means the talent is compartmentalised away from games, Shawn explains, and that means the Malaysian games scene is still less interesting than it could be.

I ask about the games made with grants, but Shawn says he doesn't think there have been many independent developers who have managed to ship something that is comparable to the standard of indie games in the west, and even fewer indie developers in Malaysia have put something out on Steam.

'I really wanted to go to the Tokyo Game Show. I mean, who wouldn't want to go to the Tokyo Game Show? I mean, I'm a gamer,' he says. 'But it would also be a nice opportunity to show Velocibox.'

'And what did you get out of it?' I ask.

'Nothing much.' Shawn shrugs. 'I saw a lot of publishers, but they were mostly interested in mobile games.'

He tells me he did get one thing out of it though: he made friends with Willy Chyr, developer of Relativity, an exploration game in an Escher-like world. He got some interesting feedback from him. But I have a hunch about this: as much as Shawn thinks that this is incidental, I know that

Willy knows Brendon Chung, a subject of one of my earlier Embed with's, and this means that should Shawn need help or advice or a place to stay for a festival in the USA, this is a ready-made network he will need or want.

Shawn hasn't got much coverage yet for Velocibox, and he once told me he doesn't mind being in Malaysia away from the indie centre of the USA because the internet makes anything possible. But part of me squeaks in a small voice: if people meet you and like you, they're more likely to play your game, be they consumer, developer, journalist. Meeting someone is powerful stuff.

Really, this is why you go to conventions. This is why you go to TGS. Human charisma alone is powerful enough to make even the stoniest person play the shittiest game. And Shawn has plenty of charisma, and his game is good, even if it's the sort of thing I'd never play in case I flung a peripheral through a car window.

The way to make it into people's lives and stay there is to be remembered, and really, I feel like me and my byline know this lesson the best.

I think Shawn will make it. He's got the chops.

*

I walk home after dark along the Odakyu trainline. Pure espresso rushes my veins. No one is around. The air feels clean and cold; a line of bulbous neat-clipped trees that surround a house seem to gleam like emeralds.

My eyes are clear, my nails are long, the navy Tokyo sky is taut above me, and I could scratch a gash straight through it and I can feel myself grinning. The sort of grin that might scare another mammal.

Grasshoppers start to sing out in the residential gardens of Setagaya ku; I finally realise the feeling on my skin.

It is the feeling of being home.

It is the feeling of knowing the language. It is the feeling of sliding into an old, loved pair of jeans. It is the feeling of relief. I know this place. I know it well.

I made it halfway around the world to my old home. I fucking made it all the way across the world with only writing to show. I fucking made it and I didn't fold and I didn't fuck it all up and I wrote things I was proud of, and here it is, the midnight Tokyo sky like it was dry cleaned and brushed for my arrival, every iced coffee delicately prepared, every train on time, every escalator primed with the shrill voice of welcome. I remember the mistakes I made here last time, the green of my twenties, the izakayas I lurked in, the nihon shu shots, the terrible one-night stands, the Chiba palm trees, the Kichijoji cemetery, the Asakusa public baths, the hoarse Shinjuku karaoke, Dogenzaka love hotel silence, Womb's lights and lasers and heartbeat. I made it back here. I made it. I fucking made it, and it feels like being newborn single for the first time in five years, just like then. Just like then.

For the past ten days, every Tokyo night has sounded like Nicki Minaj sang it.

I'll be twenty-nine today in this survival horror of life, and all I want you to do is put your drinks up, Tokyo. Put your drinks up. Put your drinks up.

Embed with ...
Ojiro Fumoto

Ojiro's view from Pico Pico Café

I went to Tokyo to look for a Japanese independent gamemaker who is trying to change the cultural landscape. Lurking in a Tokyo Indies meetup, I found Ojiro Fumoto and initially wrote about him for The Guardian *but ... I didn't know then how much momentum twenty-two-year-old Ojiro had.*

The Tokyo sky is gorged on Nintendo pink-white clouds, I cut alongside the silver *mama charis* locked up by Soshigaya Okura station. My heart lies like a lozenge on my tongue. There's Santigold in my ears and I'm going to meet Ojiro at Ueno station to buy him lunch. I'm going to ask him about his game, Downwell.

At a Tokyo Indies meetup in Shibuya weeks before, I'd stumbled in expecting a throng of Japanese faces, but instead the diversity of the crowd surprised me – mainly because the Tokyo Game Show had invited many independent developers over from the west to populate the Sony-sponsored indie stands.

But that's not to say there weren't Japanese developers at Tokyo Indies. Among others, Ojiro turned up to show his game Downwell, a vertical-orientated roguelike for mobile that he is making in Gamemaker.

'You go down a well with guns for shoes,' Ojiro said, the literal nature of the title making him grin.

Downwell was responsive, effervescent to witness. Pissing off the shopkeeper in his game solicited loud laughter from the assembled developers as he roamed to smack the player character in the face. It's easy to pick up and play: one tap to jump and another to shoot bullets from your shoes. The environment is pleasingly destructible: things pop apart and trash themselves; collecting things is pleasant. The slide of the jump and the resistance in the air as you shoot the objects below feels good. Enemy animations are funny, cute. The black, white and red graphics have an archaic, genteel feel about them, like Downwell belongs on a BBC Micro, a NES, or an original chunky grey Gameboy.

You can feel it stroking a little something in your attention – that core of you that craves overcoming a problem your mind has solved but your hands have not yet mastered. The urge to clean up. To tidy. To scrape the levels clean of their Stuff.

A week later I put <u>Downwell in The Guardian.</u> Devolver emailed Ojiro to ask if they could publish his game and offered him a large sum of money.

*

I hesitate. 'Was that ... because I wrote about it?' I ask Ojiro, about Devolver publishing him.

We are walking through rainy Ueno streets weeks later. He says he thinks so.

I'm in shock. I didn't think I had that sort of power: the power to give someone a publisher.

I've never thought hard about my 'readership'. I never ask about numbers or hits and I try not to look at my Patreon backers or how much I'm being pledged (because I am scared of measuring myself). I write what I want how I want.

Of course I thought I had *power*, but emotional power. You know, making someone sob at my trite experience of Gone Home, giving someone a thrillride, or just making someone laugh through observation. A little readership of people who like to be moved. You never think about the link between poverty and press coverage until you one day dramatically influence it.

There is a responsibility to cover poor, talented developers whose work you personally love. It is your responsibility to find these people and to dissect why their work is good, where it comes from. Everyone benefits from originality and perspective, and the developer gets to eat at the end of it.

For the first time I feel a bit like I have vertigo. I know real journalists, I think. They do not look like me and they cannot really feel like this much of a fraud. The capital J Journalists I know are older men with awards and perfunctory Twitter accounts that discuss no feelings. I'd describe them as professional. No one has ever, and will ever, describe me as professional.

'Someone told me about how big *The Guardian* is,' Ojiro says to me about the article I wrote. 'I'd never heard of it.'

'I guess it *is* big,' I say, raising eyebrows. 'I guess it is.'

Ojiro

146

Ojiro-san takes me to a place near Ueno station that sells cow tongue for lunch – it's a popular place, and you can get a set. I love lunch sets in Japan: you always get rice, soup and pickles or some sort of salad.

We speak in English – Ojiro spent his childhood in New Zealand when his mother separated from his father and wanted to live in an English-speaking country for a while to test out her English.

'Nice phone by the way,' he says. (I smashed my phone screen up in Malaysia getting out of a taxi drunk.) I grin and say I should get it fixed.

'When do you get time to develop Downwell?' I ask, as the waitress delivers our food. Ojiro's in his final year at Tokyo University of the Arts. He told me on the way here he is studying opera singing, one of the rare times any game developer has ever expressed an interest in opera.

'I don't have many classes. I spend most of my time developing. I have lots of freedom since I'm not married or anything. I don't have much money but I don't need much money either. I think I decided at a good time to become a game developer.'

Shop in Downwell

'Why did you start to make games?'

'Braid and Super Meat Boy – those days when indie games got super popular. I've been playing games since then. I was even playing Cave Story and stuff before then. I've always loved indie games and dreamed of making games for myself. But I always imagined that programming would be way too hard for me.'

'That's the biggest barrier, right?' I say. 'Everyone thinks that.'

'Yeah, and I just gave up on it before even trying. But then I entered school and I was singing in front of people. I've always had this, "Why the hell am I singing?" It's so ridiculous. I'm Japanese, I'm pretending to be this Italian young boy who's in love with one girl ... I'm singing about my love for her ... That's not what I wanted to do. I thought hard about what I really wanted to do. If I could do anything in the world what would I do? I didn't want to become the greatest thing in the world. I wanted to become a game developer. So I started studying really hard. I used Gamemaker Studio. It turned out to be quite easy to use. So I've only been making games since then.'

'For how many years?'

'I only started this March.'

Uh. 'That's incredible,' I say. 'You've got the hang of it ... pretty quick.'

'I've always had this game design stuff in my head. Just never actually used it,' Ojiro says, as if making a game like this was just like falling off a log.

'I don't think I've met many people in Japan who play western indie games,' I say. 'Maybe doujin games like Cave Story, but how did you hear about stuff like Braid?'

'I lived in New Zealand for five years from when I was ten until I was fifteen. And while indie games weren't that big back then – I was playing Half-Life 2 or Unreal Tournament – when I came back to Japan I bought an Xbox 360. I'd never liked the Japanese "animation girl" games. I never liked those. I thought it was ridiculous that people liked those games. I kept playing the western stuff – reading up on the western gaming websites. That's why I play all the popular games from the west.'

'Did you ever talk about those games with your friends at school?' I ask, curious as to how popular western indie games might be in Japan. It seems like PC gaming isn't a thing and Microsoft never had much luck selling consoles here.

'No. There was just one guy who had the same taste as me. I played those games with him. But no one else. Just me and that guy.'

'So they're really not popular here at all.'

'No.' Ojiro shakes his head. 'No one even knows about Steam. It's getting a bit more popular these days but … It's really unfortunate, Japanese gamers don't really focus on good game design. Instead they focus on girls.'

'Do they really?'

'They do. As you wrote in your article, there is a doujin community making games, but they don't really focus much on game design, instead they focus on the costume of the character. And the companies you mentioned, the games you mentioned earlier – Dark Souls, Platinum Games – they are the exception in the Japanese game industry, I think. They actually challenge and make new stuff. But most of the companies spend a lot of money on character design. Not much on new design. But they make money in Japan. Those really shallow designs.'

I am surprised that Ojiro is as hard on Japan as he is, but he's not alone in criticising the Japanese game industry this way. Keiji Inafune, famous for creating Megaman, has been much harsher on the industry's perceived stagnancy in the past.

I ask if I can play the Downwell build on Ojiro's phone.

'It's semi-randomly generated and it doesn't get saved,' he

explains, as I smash up stuff with my gunboots. 'If you die you start from scratch. It has upgrades like Spelunky. It's not as deep as those games yet. I managed to build the basics of the game now. From then I just have to keep adding content – adding enemies.'

'What are these? Snowmen?'

'Jizos,' Ojiro says. 'Haven't you seen Jizos? Jizo statues are these statues that you see around town. They are said to suck in bad things. Like ... bad blood. And sickness. They're good luck.'

'Is that what they mean in the game?'

'Nah, they're just like, shopkeepers,' he says.

'Does the player character have a name?'

'Nope. Nameless. And genderless too.'

There's no music in the game yet, so I suggest Ojiro sings some opera for the soundtrack. He seems not to think this is a good idea.

*

A lot of visitors say that Tokyo is the '*Bladerunner* city', but that feels wrong. Shanghai or Hong Kong fit that bill better. Tokyo is organised, more regulated. There's little that's dishevelled about Tokyo compared to most other sprawling cities. London looks like shit next to Tokyo's clipped topiary, trashless pavements and trains that are only ever late by a matter of seconds even in an earthquake.

But there's some anarchy left.

Kabuki-cho in Shinjuku used to be the capital of sleaze, massage parlours, Yakuza-run soaplands, cafés with mirror floors, porn shops – my western male friends used to get solicited everywhere we went. In the years since I left Japan it seems to have been rinsed with medicated boring, which is really disappointing to my sleazy sensibilities. Less sex on display means much less foot traffic.

But it's still got a little gem of a good time.

The Golden Gai is the last offshoot of the raging party. It's a collection of tiny, narrow pre-war streets that house dozens of little cubicle bars, most of which can really only fit up to six people at a time. Everyone has a favourite bar here, but I try a different one every time.

If you want a little of the oden-steamed warm breath and lanterns, you can jam yourself in the back of a bar here with some strangers and mangle your Japanese conversation into a stupor.

Ojiro has been readying his game for the IGF all this week, and I'm getting antsy. Without him I drag western friends down the little backstreets, looking for trouble.

Strange things always happen to me in the Golden Gai. Stay after the trains have stopped, and things start to happen. There's an excess of energy that ends up there. It's a magic born of the compulsory intimacy of touching elbows in the tiny box bars that live on these little claustrophobic streets. It's the same kind of magic that flows in the Old Town of Edinburgh: vennel chat, gregarious friendships, the sharing of overspill cigarettes and early hours drunk. People want to talk. They need to.

We stray into a cubbyhole where a handsome woman with Sephiroth hair is tending bar. We ask if it's okay if gaijin take up space; she nods and tells us the cover charge. I nudge the Japanese guys next to me and begin chatting in Japanese, but soon they get cocky and we all start speaking English. It turns out they're going to a club night tonight: one of the guys, the suave one with the long hair chain smoking, owns a record label. He grins at us. 'We're going to Shinjuku Loft for Seapunk,' he cackles. 'You should come!'

We down the rest of our beer and follow them out of the bar. They trail us all around Kabuki-cho, making a maze of the streets until somehow, somehow, we end up in the green room in the back of Shinjuku Loft (in a basement), the bands all scrambling for cables and getting drunk on conbini beer.

No one knows who we are but they all seem not to give a fuck. Nature Danger Gang is playing. We hang out chatting backstage until things get blurry.

This is Tokyo.

Backstage at Tokyo Loft

Ojiro and I walk to his apartment in Ueno. It's rainy and cold for the first time in a while. I ask him what his girlfriend thinks of his plans to make games.

'I told her I didn't want to work for a company, I just wanted to make my own games,' he says. 'Japanese people think that getting into a company and working their arses off for their entire lives is a good thing for them, to have stable income. But doing something that you don't wanna do for the rest of your life just for a stable income is not my idea of a happy life. But most Japanese think that way.

'My girlfriend was sort of surprised when I told her.

When you wrote that article, and when other people started writing articles ... I guess her worry lessened a bit.'

Ojiro's workstation at home

Ojiro has a very small apartment with just enough room for a large TV, a bookshelf, a bed, a small kitchen and a tiny bathroom. His desk sits at the end of his bed, and this is where he's making Downwell.

Ojiro says he initially just wanted to make Spelunky for smartphones, just because he wanted to play that game. He wants to release it in the west and in Japan in Japanese, but he doesn't think it will do well in Japan. 'There would surely be some audience, but mostly people want a cute anime girl. Maybe if I make the character a girl. DLC costumes or something...'

Ojiro's just making assets now, drawing new enemies. He talks about these for a while, until he slides into what really made him start making games.

'So, Rami Ismail wrote an article on <u>Game A Week</u>,' Ojiro begins.

This article was a personal blog on Gamasutra about how the Vlambeer developer and his partner at the company JW became better developers through failure – sheer volume of prototypes giving them the design experience they needed to succeed.

'When I read that I was like, oh wow,' Ojiro says. 'And I love Rami Ismail. I loved Vlambeer from the start. I was really inspired by that. I started making a game a week from March. I made all these small games. I'd been making games for like twelve weeks. I made twelve really shitty games. And for my thirteenth game I came upon the idea of infinite faller. And this game turned out to be quite decent. So I decided to work on it for more than a week. And that's where I'm at now.

'While I was doing this game-a-week thing I found it took quite a bit of time to draw graphical assets. So that's why I decided to make it black and white. Other games I made during that game a week ... I kept on simplifying the graphics, the colour palettes. I like the black-and-white stuff, and it took much less time.'

I say it looks retro, reminds me of NES days.

'People tell me that!' Ojiro says. 'They talk about MSX games. I've never played any. The games I played were like SNES days.'

'It reminds me a bit of Gauntlet, maybe,' I say. 'Gauntlet II used to have this voice if you were running out of food: "RED WARRIOR NEEDS FOOD BADLY."'

With glee, I show him Gauntlet II on Steam. The sound effects are glorious. Ojiro can't make out what the voices are saying but he seems to love it. I get excited for the first time about being an 'older generation' gamer than someone else.

Tokyo Grand Hyatt martini

It's late, and I'm sitting in a shady Shimokitazawa bar with Jake Adelstein – the infamous yakuza journalist from Missouri – while he smokes and I pay for cocktails. I had to coax him out with money because of that old journo problem, the Late Payment. There's a breaking story he thinks he might have to work: ebola is suspected to have reached Japan. A well-known journalist was screened for it at Haneda.

'The cat is on the roof,' Jake says, darkly.

'What?'

'It's this old story about giving bad news,' Jake says. 'A man calls home and asks his wife how the children are. His wife says that they're fine, they're in bed, all the laundry's done, stuff like that ... Also the cat is dead.'

In Jake's story the man is perturbed at his wife's bluntness and tells her to make it a softer blow. 'Maybe three calls – the first time just say the cat is on the roof, the second time say, oh, the cat is injured, we took it to the vet, and then maybe tell me the cat is dead.

'But the next day the man's wife phones him up and says, "Your mother's on the roof!"'

The Tokyo Vice author shakes the bench laughing.

I'm due to go on Giant Bomb at 1 a.m. so I go back to Jake's house where he has superior internet, expensive sake, and a quiet room to sit in. We talk for a long time about the era of games he used to report on working at a newspaper – System Shock 2, Deus Ex, Thief. He loved those games. Then he became a real journalist. The fear of death stopped being virtual and started being very real.

I'm not sure how we got around to it, but we start to talk about journalistic ethics. Jake ignores other ideas of journalistic 'ethics' and has his own code:

1. get the truth by any means possible;
2. get the story out;
3. protect your sources;

4. if you can't do C, then don't do B. Retreat and figure out a better way.

'I slept with sources, blackmailed people, raided rubbish bins, traded massages for tips,' Jake says of his years of working as a Tokyo police reporter on the most dangerous beat – organised crime. He tells me no one has ever hauled him up for any of those methods. He says he's aware that if he was a woman he'd be called manipulative, a conniving bitch. But most seem content to paint him as a lovable rogue. The worst accusations seem to be that he's a CIA operative, spying on Japan, which suggests that even his enemies suspect him of some competency.

It's tempting to think that Jake gets off on danger, but I don't think he does. I think he likes control: the ability to control his situation, everyone in it. He said no to Afghanistan and no to ebola reportage in Africa. 'I couldn't speak the language,' he said of Afghanistan, 'and you can't bargain with a deadly disease.'

'Responsible'

Jake puts me in a spare room at the top of the house, and gives me a T-shirt to sleep in. It says 'responsible'. It's not a T-shirt he wants any more, it doesn't suit me, but I haven't seen a bed since Malaysia so I promptly fall asleep in it.

My friend Justin, who reports on Japan for *The Guardian*, texts Jake later. It must have been a somewhat chiding message about plying me with good sake and trying out Aikido moves on me, because when we go to get an Irish coffee the next day, Jake says, 'Tell him I was a perfect gentleman, huh?'

Jake's pretty upstanding for a guy who blackmails and sleeps with sources. As far as I know he's still alive and reads my articles about scary videogames on Vice.

*

I catch up with Ojiro finally in Pico Pico Café, a video game-themed café and workspace. He's trying to put together a menu screen of sorts, and the co-owner of the café, Joseph White, is helping with some of the design issues.

Ojiro says he's decided to drop out of university. He says he had to convince his parents that even if he fails to make it with this game, he could get a job at a bigger games company with the prototypes he's made.

I ask him what his girlfriend thinks of this.

'Actually, she broke up with me,' he says. 'I told her I was dropping out of school because of game stuff – the exams were taking up too much time. She didn't seem like she wanted that ... We broke up.'

Ojiro doesn't seem happy about the breakup, but he doesn't seem preoccupied with it. He tells me that he's been thinking about his future a lot. I think he's making plans. He said he hopes that if he has any success at all, that other Japanese developers might also follow the indie path, try to make it on their own, instead of being absorbed into the increasingly sequel-driven studio system. He wants to move to Kyoto for the cheap rent and make games for the rest of his life.

If anything, the cat is not on the roof. Ojiro's push for recognition is the most exciting thing I've witnessed: the birth of a new generation of Japanese creators.

I type this to you from Kagoshima, my old volcano-adjacent home in Kyushu, where *You Only Live Twice* was filmed.

Tokyo seems fast, crushed, overexposed in my head, a blur of conbini coffee, yakitori and wine, Odakyu line trains and trains, the Park Hyatt jazz trio, a manfriend humming in his sleep by the glow of love hotel light switches, Star Bar in Shinjuku crammed with video game trinkets. Tokyo was good to me.

I've made it back here for a few days before leaving for Singapore. I intend to see my old Iaido sensei, tell him I still have my practice sword. The rice fields that went by on my bus trip from the airport were all familiar; I became an adult in the shadow of the twice-daily explosions of the hot volcano in the bay. If anything, Japan taught me to be accommodating, flexible, considerate, and to carry a big katana.

And if you can't do that, well, maybe you can make someone proud.

My luggage in a tatami room in Kagoshima City, Kagoshima Prefecture

Embed with ...
Singapore

Gwen Guo

Landing in Singapore with a purple bob is enough to make me aware that I look like a nineties drug dealer, and not for the first time. As I am patted down and scanned before I get to leave the baggage claim, I grin at Brian Kwek and Ian Gregory of Witching Hour Studios, my two generous hosts for a whirlwind week in the gracious city state where they live and work.

Due to my hosts' limited time I've got about four days to crush into my brain how they think about games.

I'm on the tail end of my journey. I've only got Australia to go, and I'm starting to get weary, feel overexposed. I keep thinking of my mind as being composed of photographic paper, and there always seems to be no room left on it for images to be drawn. But each time I surprise myself: Singapore is beautiful. By night it seems the most likely candidate for a futuristic city state: it hangs between dystopia and utopia in an entrancing way. Laws here are strictly enforced, though, Brian tells me, not as strictly as I'd think. Just as I arrive, Brian tells me hookahs are getting banned (probably because the government can't find a good way to tax them) though no one seems particularly annoyed about this.

I came straight from the impending winter of Japan, so I am wearing too many layers of clothing and Singapore's humid air hits by the car doors. Brian grins at me and asks me if I'm hungry. I nod enthusiastically.

Gwen Guolan driving me to Chinese massage

By many accounts I am not actually worthy of how friendly and funny and personable Brian and Ian are: they take me straight to a covered outdoor food market by the shore and buy at least five dishes, all of which are delicious. I dip chopsticks in plates of shellfish in a sweet sauce, some sort of pig intestine in sticky black sauce, pull meat off satay skewers. It's all accompanied by this huge glass of cold pressed sugarcane drink, which will mark almost every meal.

Over dinner Ian and I talk about the government funding that is available to Singaporean game developers: much of the problem, he says, lies in the fact that the government funds things that promote their own agenda and are not necessarily what's best for the makers. Ian explains that games that are explicitly made about traditional Singapore culture often don't speak to him: he may be from Singapore, but the comics and fantasy literature books he grew up with from across the world shaped how he thinks about the world around him. Our global culture has helped to give him an outlook that is not only Singaporean, but has all the touchstones of participation in a bigger cultural conversation.

I say that I think we are talking about parochial meanings and universal meanings, and use of both together can be interesting.

Ian and Brian say when someone like Barack Obama visits, and Singapore can present a game as emblematic of the creative output of the local community, they'll know they have been successful.

We talk about how we'd like to see more politics in games. 'Games are, at the end of the day, conflict,' Ian says. 'And politics are also conflict. A lot of people say they don't want politics in their games because they don't want to take a position. Everything in a game comes from somewhere though – it's fear of scrutiny.'

'They want only the politics they are familiar with,' Brian says.

'I believe in dictatorships,' Ian says. 'I like Lee Kwan Yew. I like the fact that one person can make all the right decisions, versus a group of people given the power ... I believe that when you put more people together the IQ just drops.'

'You think compromise is weakening everything?' I ask.

'No one can guarantee what qualities a dictator has,' Ian says. 'Everywhere there are good examples and bad examples. We are lucky to exist in a place where it's good. We are technically the same as North Korea. Dictatorship is successful when you're lucky enough to have the right person in power.'

We go on to talk about Singapore's history. 'Singapore is majority Chinese.' Ian describes the tensions that existed when Singapore was part of the Malaysian federation. My observations of Malaysian life while hanging with Cass are put into relief: Ian and Brian seem very aware of the racial tensions of Malaysia because of Singapore's separation from the Federation almost fifty years ago. Here in Singapore there seems to be a much more comfortable emphasis on Chinese heritage, although many people around me affectionately joke about how Brian's Chinese reading ability is not as good as his parents would like.

We go to dinner the next night, and I meet some of the game developers Ian and Brian are familiar with. There's a real feel of a New Generation in the conversation, so strong I keep having these weird images of *Wayne's World* jokes about Pepsi appear in my vision. I get the impression that everyone present is drifting away from the 'old Singapore' that people might associate with their parents' generation, and it's replaced by a feeling of chasing something, a feeling of being excited about the future and creating a new idea of Singapore's relationship with technology. The cultural heritage of Singapore is respected, but at the same time there's this overwhelming feeling, as we lean over cold ale and chatter in an overloud manner to each other, that something new is being belligerently carved out in the wake of Singapore's first gaming convention, Gamestart 2014. It's really exciting to be around people who seem in charge of this future.

The little café bar we are in is modern and has adorable, almost Lichtenstein-esque art on the walls, and I'm sitting opposite Teck Lee Tan, who keeps completely befuddling me with his voice. He sounds almost exactly like Chris Remo when he speaks to me. I make him say Idle Thumbs jokes into my phone for posterity. Later he'll tell me that he saw a grandmother driving around in a Lamborghini once, which sounds like the most Singapore of things.

Gwen and some ladies

162

It's here that I also meet Gwen Guo. Gwen is exuberant and filthy-mouthed in the exact same way that both me and PC Doris Thatcher from Hot Fuzz are. We sit next to each other and get along immediately. She mentions some movie star she would like to paw and caress, and I am immediately on board. Gwen has an infectious laugh too, like it comes from her whole body, and a smile that acts like a lighthouse lamp when it shines in your eyes.

Gwen is an alumna of the Singapore MIT Gambit Lab, and she's a talented audio designer for her own company, <u>IMBA Interactive</u>, as well as a man fancier. She did some of the audio for the first Singaporean indie game on PS4, <u>One Upon Light</u>, a gorgeous top–down puzzler in black and white.

Gwen is quite into telling me about her inflatable cow, which has an orifice in its behind for reasons I will only tell to people who buy me a drink in the pub.

We play D&D one night, before Ian's grandmother serves up the most delicious prawn laksa I have ever tasted.

*

NO DURIANS NO SMOKING

There's a languid pleasure in waiting. The feeling of being suspended. You might look down, sometimes, and think that you are far from the ground, like you might drop if you didn't fly so hard. You might become scared of what might happen. But if you look back in front of you, where there is clear sky, where you can see the obstacles coming and you take them one at a time, it's like waiting, not moving. It's like suddenly becoming aware that you are alive.

Is waiting when we are most alive?

Mostly, this job entails becoming a human sponge, a person that other people put their imprint on – or this is who I would like to become. Something that other people affect, something that cannot become tired or lonely. Something that can reflect back some of the resonance of what creating is. But humans cannot become objects. Humans are the subjects.

I wait for little ideas to prick my skin and show blood. But isn't this what I did before? Before, when I felt more allowed to talk about my feelings with others, with friends, it was an outward motion, but it was still waiting of a kind.

Perhaps waiting is the act of a lost person. But sometimes you can be pointedly, very … lost.

Brian takes me for lunch at Wah Kee Big Prawn Noodles, where we pay 10c more for our pressed sugar cane drinks to have less ice in them, and then we drive to Haw Par Villa.

Originally Tiger Balm Gardens, Haw Par Villa is a theme park that was constructed in 1937 by Burmese-Chinese brothers Aw Boon Haw and Aw Boon Par. They invented Tiger Balm. They had way too much money. They decided to construct this place to teach traditional Chinese values. When the Singapore Tourist Board took it over, they ran it somewhat disastrously, and it has since become free to visit the park.

But through all that history and monetary difficulty it has become rundown. Perhaps in its heyday it had rides or working fountains, some signs of life, but when me and Brian get there it's almost deserted. The concrete and fibreglass statues' bright primary colours are peeling. The Monkey God looks fucked off and worn, mid-fight with his enemy. I can imagine, by way of daydream in the hot Singapore sun, that when this park opened it was like being in a striking tapestry of Chinese history, where the tales of the Monkey God and the huge battles of Chinese tradition must have been alternately entrancing and terrifying for tiny children. It is still full of delight and terror, though for me, a different kind of terror.

As the paint has faded and become water-stained, as the water features have stopped functioning, as the sad, defunct open-air theatres and idle, menacing displays have become wistful, you start to think about how technology might be so obsessed with the onward march of time that it is destroying itself.

I begin to realise, as Brian and I enter the cave of the Ten Courts of Hell, where all sorts of punishments are meted out to wretched plaster-and-wire models, that Brian has forgotten almost everything about his visit here when he was young. He remembers it being a ride, a water ride into the dark, a terrifying sort of existential meeting-your-own-doom sort of thing, where there is no water now, and you can stare as long as you like at a little anguished model having his flesh burned off or at spikes being driven into a plaster man's asshole. Brian remembers it being a lot more terrifying, he tells me. But I can imagine the sort of terror younger Brian felt at all of this: it is meant to scare as much as it is meant to instruct. Sinners' guts are apparently ripped out for cheating on exams, according to Chinese and Taoist hell, and other such minor infractions are as harshly dealt with.

Now, the whole thing seems like the sort of dream you might have after too much absinthe: abstract and with odd shadows from half-light. The exhibits haven't been looked after the way you would like, and sometimes you have to squint to make out whether the sinner's legs have been chopped off, or if they have merely crumbled, disintegrated, fallen off after years of rainwater, storms, humidity and simple old age. Sometimes the signs that tell you what is happening in the static, fusty displays are not attached to the correct ones, so that you stare for a long time trying to make out, in the dark, if the person is really dying of what the display is telling you.

You end up wondering if a sinner's torture is all in their imagination.

Brian and I talk about the similarity between theme park designers and game designers, but we drift into the idea of the Monomyth, or hero's journey, and what games have taught him about it. Brian says he learned a lot about the Monomyth from Metal Gear Solid games. He explains that a narrative from the hundreds of characters in these Chinese traditional myths seems inextricable now that he is looking at a visual representation of them in a park.

I feel sad about this. I feel like games are empty of the kind of narratives these Chinese traditional worlds represent. Perhaps in some manner I could see Haw Par Villa having something in common with Deadly Premonition, but it focuses mainly on one detective rather than many characters' interwoven stories. Perhaps, I think, fighting games are actually video games' way of approaching Chinese myth, with hundreds of characters in the canon, each with an intricacy, an interlocking narrative with countless others.

It might sound like complaining, to say that Haw Par Villa is run down, but I love it just as I found it. It was like a prolonged embodiment of the cartoon horror part of the Disney film *Pinocchio*, with the lost children and the donkey ears, a lost, absurd wonderland, and I think I said so to Brian and Ian in the Witching Hour offices. It was rich with the sort of reflection on life and death that I doubt the west has ever approached in a theme park.

Witching Hour is interested in constructing worlds, and there's a lot of energy thrown at trying to find new fantasy environments in which to place Brian and Ian's characters. Their current project, Masquerada: Songs and Shadows, a fantasy RPG, seems well thought out – it reminds me of a slightly quirkier Neverwinter Nights – but there's a lot of little projects the studio have worked on that impress me. In particular, I liked this little strategy game, Witching Hour made on their off time between projects. It's a thing called Romans In My Carpet!

The current thing that is weighing on Ian's mind is his gay character in Masquerada: Songs and Shadows. He is a gay ally in a city state where male-on-male sexual activity is illegal. Category 302 of the penal code places homosexuals and transvestites in the same category as paedophiles. The law seems particularly preoccupied with whether men are behaving 'effeminately' or not.

Ian tells me he thinks that in the media at large there is a curious preoccupation with gay people's sex lives, something that he thinks is unfair and shouldn't define gay people or fictional gay characters. Though he is straight, he tells me he wants to write a gay character that isn't defined by sex.

I ask him if he will get in trouble with the government for writing such a narrative into his game.

'I hope so,' he says.

*

There's a steady community that Ian and Brian are a part of that they could easily grow into something more social, if they wanted to. Brian and I talked about London's Wild Rumpus scene and how I thought it would work well in Singapore, given spaces like the café bar we went to. There's a kind of restlessness in them both, the sort of restlessness that comes with having a studio that employs a small group of people, and the pressure that comes from wanting so badly to give them a beneficial creative atmosphere to work in. There's that tension of wanting to create something new and great, but also wanting to be able to pay people, and pay themselves. It's something that many of the creators I've covered before only had to worry about for themselves, but Ian and Brian lay the sense of responsibility out raw. They often grill me for ideas about how to improve their game, how to interest people, how to involve prospective players. But the truth is it seems half witchcraft to me too. It's a combination of wanting to make something and that something being something someone wants to buy and presenting that something as palatable. I guess later Frank Lantz at NYU would have a better diagram for that.

That familiar fret, the one where you wonder whether you are the sponge or the paint, comes back, and as far as business advice goes, I know I am not configured for that yet.

Frank Lantz advice

I fell asleep, and therefore, so did my character, in the last battle of Dungeons and Dragons with my Singapore crew – and Ian is probably the best dungeon master I've ever gamed with, so it's no reflection on him. It's becoming so that I can fall asleep practically anywhere at any time now. I count up my achievements as I come to my final stop: Australia.

1. Can sleep on practically any surface;
2. In a cacophonic battle for the fate of the world, I would rather fall asleep in a nearby bush with some beer;
3. Can walk through the Ten Courts of Hell and survive.

But that last one belongs to humans at large, if 2014 has anything at all to show to us. Hell is negotiable.

Me at the gates of Chinese hell

Embed with ...
Marigold Bartlett and
Christy Dena

Magister Ludi on show at Experimenta media exhibition,
Melbourne

It seems only fair that here comes the rush of adrenaline, now
that I know what I'm doing. The destination is Australia: I'm
stuck in LAX, the world's second worst airport, Christmas
is coming, a woman has been taken off the plane with an
allergic reaction to something she ate in the tinsel-draped
choo-choo train-lined terminal. I am flung into my final
month to a burst of sugary pop music.

I look down at my hands and they are shaking with
anticipation.

It isn't because I drank a gallon of fructose-packed
smoothie in the world's second worst airport. It isn't because
I took any drugs (though, God, America has a love affair with
melatonin which is banned in the EU). It's because I am at
the peak of the graph.

No one bothers to go to Australia. They might go to video
games' motherland, Japan, but no games journalist goes to
Australia. Why would you go to Australia? Australians come
to us. We do not go to them.

It's where Katharine Neil helped set up Freeplay,

the independent games festival. It's where Escape From Woomera came from, the Half-Life mod that made the *New York Times* sit up and notice games for creating a full-blown argument in the Australian parliament, the game that forced the public to ask 'Are games art? Are games political?' way back in the haze of time. It wouldn't be a narrative if I didn't start seeing my path lead back on itself. It's happening now. When I stayed with Katharine back in April I had only a thin line of a pattern sewn; now it's a tapestry. A fucking tapestry.

Qantas show a selection of Australian movies (including the fairly dreadful movie *Australia*, which is only notable for Hugh Jackman pouring a bucket of water over his naked body, the reason straight women and gay men should care about *Australia*). I somewhat stubbornly watch *Grease*, which is Australian only because Olivia Newton-John is.

Wonder what she's doing now.

Melbourne

I land in Melbourne with a giant scarf on that I bought in Brooklyn and is so warm that when I meet Brendan Keogh and Helen Berents, my fixers for the month, they laugh at my underslept bewilderment at the heat.

Brendan and Helen have a place in Melbourne near Pentridge Gaol, where Ned Kelly, the bushranger, outlaw and controversial Australian hero, was imprisoned. When we arrive it seems strange that it is such a quaint, quiet place now, the daunting history dampened by palm trees and coffee shops next to the tall lookout that presumably overlooked Kelly's last days. Strange to think also, that Australia's colonial history means that this building is not the ancient behemoth my Scottish brain presumes: it was built in 1850 and shut in 1997 – young in UK terms.

Important to bring Coburg Lager to parties

It's December summer and dry hot. It feels like my Celtic skin is burning with every touch of the sun when I leave the car to bring my two fat travel bags indoors. There is a fragrance outdoors that will take me a few days to interpret. It is making connections between neurons; they spark a lot and wander until I understand that the smell of Australia is the smell of every bourgeois organic beauty shop in the UK. It's the smell of pale green eucalyptus trees, their spindly limbs rising like jagged fingers towards the sky. Koala bears, though none live around here, supposedly get high on eucalyptus and hang around all day looking smug.

I am sleepy with beer to the sound of the Melbourne games community playing Mario Kart in the living room. Brendan, a games critic and academic, knows everyone, and it's how we met – one Games Developers Conference we were drunk in many San Francisco bars together. I'd wager most journalists share bars in common, though they don't all drink alcohol.

The kid prodigy Harry Lee, creator of Stickets, is here. And the creators of Push Me Pull You, Jake Strasser, Michael

McMaster, Stuart Gillespie-Cook and Nico Disseldorp have brought a build of their squeaky little local co-op game. Push Me Pull You feels like a Bennett Foddy game (also an Australian, though he is now resident in New York) such as Poleriders, and might be (controversially) even more fun to play.

The artist Marigold Bartlett, affectionately known as Goldie, is here too. Goldie is a little shy to begin with, but we will get to know each other. I heard about her work via Parallels: The Freeplay 2014 Showcase, featuring nine innovative and original Australian video game projects that Dan Golding, now the director of Freeplay, had selected to show.

In conjunction with the designer and writer Christy Dena, sound designer and composer Trevor Dikes, and the programmer Cameron Owen, Goldie produced the art for the tablet game Magister Ludi, an 'escape the room game with a twist'. Goldie's work on that game looks like this:

Screenshot from Magister Ludi

More on Magister Ludi later.

Much of the early days in Melbourne are a jetlagged blur. I go for beers at Trent Kuster's flat one night. Trent is the chair of the Freeplay festival and the creative lead on Armello, a strategy game that Trent tells me with a giant grin is 'popular with furries'. You might remember Trent from when I wrote about Adriaan in Amsterdam: he is the guy in the club with

Tall Hot Girl, and I guess that is how I will mostly remember him. Didn't I say we were going in loops? Didn't I say this fabric was thick?

Usually you can tell Trent from his ever-present charismatic broad smile, his curly Dutch hair, and how much he enjoys laughing. It is hard not to be impressed by how much Trent enjoys life. It is also important to note that he is somehow the face of Lynx gift sets in Australia. (That's 'Axe' for you Americans.)

Trent's Lynx gift sets?!

Trent's apartment is in this eco-building – 'deep green' apartments that have apparently won an architecture award – made of reclaimed wood. He has a balcony, and seems intensely happy about it.

The author, journalist and Freeplay director Dan Golding sits to my left, who over the next few days I will come to know from his fetching collection of cable-knit jumpers (even in the heat) and his quiet, sharp intelligent way, and also his 'marvellous melange of sagely gravitas and youthful verve', and Josh Boggs, the designer of Hideo Kojima's now favourite game Framed, sits opposite, quietly chuckling at Trent's jokes.

Josh Boggs listening intently to Trent explaining something in a jumper

They teach me about strewthing a roo, beauts in utes having a bikkie, and bonzering brumbies, so I feel fairly confident everyone in Australia will understand me.

Australians have a really amiable tone of optimistic resignation about them that I admire. My favourite comment of the night comes from <u>Terry</u>, who overhears Brendan telling me about Australian Prime Minister <u>Harold Edward Holt</u>, who one day just went into the sea and never came back.

'What do you *mean* disappeared?' I exclaim over my beer.

Terry shrugs. 'We dunno where he is.'

Visiting

Helen, Brendan, Goldie, Dan and I go to visit Goldie's mum one afternoon, driving out to Werribee South, a retirement village by the sea. It's very peaceful out by the pale blue sea, and little boats bob near the shore under mottled clouds.

Goldie has these eyes that always somehow transmit severe amusement, as if they are sparking, and she always laughs at my bad jokes, which is shamelessly endearing to me. (I can't help it.)

Band photo

That's Goldie on the right. I think she is trying to point to make the picture seem like a band photo.

It's obvious where Goldie gets her enquiring mind and wide-ranging interests from as we argue animatedly about the war at the dinner table: Goldie's mother's bungalow is filled with beautiful art objects, her terrace filled with plants and paintings and things to catch the eye. There are books about history and art everywhere, and it's bright and comfortable with a view out to sea.

Goldie's mum explains to us the importance of game literacy: she says that for her generation, the idea that you might have to navigate a medium through different dimensions – three dimensions even – 'doesn't occur to you. All this [critical] thinking, no matter how good at it you are doesn't help. So you get so *furious*.'

Helen relates her first time playing games in front of Brendan, her fiancé, to us, and she says he felt like her character was playing the first person shooter genre 'in a neck brace'.

'I still remember [N64 game] Banjo Kazooie,' Goldie says. 'They put Spiral Mountain right at the very beginning. I remember it took me about twenty minutes to run up a loop, up the spiral walkway.'

'I remember that,' Dan says.

'It was teaching you to move the camera at the same time as running forward to get that turn right,' Goldie says. 'I remember moving a quarter of a centimetre forward just to get the turn right. But that was a really clever teaching tool.'

I don't know why mums love me, but they do.

Experimenta

Goldie and Christy's work on Magister Ludi was commissioned as part of the Experimenta media exhibition at the RMIT gallery, Melbourne. Experimenta is quite an existential look at how various disciplines can intertwine. It displays some spectacular work that includes this piece called Cannibal Story, which is one of the most striking animations I have ever seen. It combines traditional Putijarra storytelling (narrated by Yunkurra Billy Atkins) and animation in vibrant colours by Sohan Ariel Hayes. Goldie says she thinks the bright pinks remind her of the landscape of Australia.

Experimenta media exhibition

Magister Ludi is also here. I play it. Something about it makes me feel a kind of horrible dread, though Goldie's art is pretty and welcoming. It's something about being constrained that does it. It conveys that feeling very well.

Goldie wasn't interested in games until she was about seventeen. 'I grew up with much older brothers, so I was playing games when I was younger,' she says, over coffee, while super journalist Dan Golding listens carefully to my questions.

Goldie's boots

'But I got into digital art, moving from drawing on paper to using a tablet when I was fifteen. That led to involvement with online communities of artists. We'd just hang out online after school all evening, meeting each other and trading artwork. Then I finished high school, sat around on my bum for about three years figuring out what to do but still practising art and still playing games. I thought I could combine that and pursue that as something to study. And I wanted to stay on the tablet. I applied for RMIT and got in.

'My perception of why I wanted to go into it versus why I am in it now is so different,' Goldie explains. 'Meeting a lot of people who do the same thing as you makes you realise it's so super nuanced. I'd read somewhere when I was seventeen, if you want to go into video games, don't get too excited because you won't be making your own games, you'll be working on other people's ideas for the first twenty years.'

I say I hate that mentality. That it is the barrier to everyone making something in our medium.

'It's just not the case, either,' Goldie says. 'I'm sure it would be the case if you were "lucky" enough to get a job in triple A straight off the bat. Yes, you would be rendering floor textures for the first two years of your career. It wouldn't really allow for much exploration or growth of ideas. I just wasn't expecting to be looking at something as multi-faceted as making games.

'I really love working with constraints and in collaboration. That's the number one most exciting thing for me. I'm just out of uni – collaboration is super cool.'

Goldie thinks 'games culture' is very fragmented, but she says there is definitely a 'scene'. 'So-and-so knows so-and-so who does such-and-such, which is a problem for a lot of people who haven't experienced working amongst scenes before. Meeting people and not brown-nosing, name dropping.'

I say that I think collaboration is a better word for what we are experiencing in this arena. 'Networking' is a ruthless word that is completely inappropriate for the way games work in art scenes. It's a relationship that necessitates creatively giving in goodwill.

So how did she and Christy come to collaborate?

'I think she saw my identity design I did for Freeplay in 2013, which was my second year. That introduced me to a lot of people. That was through Harry Lee. He knew me through Sam Crisp. And he said, "I like your art." I called my mum and was pretty excited. Christy contacted me and said, "I've got this card game, it's spy-themed, I want your style, what do you reckon?" That took a hiatus for a while and then she was commissioned by Experimenta.

'She's such a good thinker, her concepts are far out, effortlessly researched. In the future I get excited about being in that stage of my career.'

Road Trip

Brendan and Helen have decided to road trip to Brisbane for Christmas and take me with them. In my brain 'road trip' just means driving for a day.

The trip from Melbourne to Brisbane to visit Christy is three days' drive.

Well, shit, I think.

But the landscape of Australia is very beautiful. It's got so many shades of yellow in it, and the sky is the biggest sky I have seen.

We drive all day to just outside Canberra, where Helen's friend is putting us up for the night.

We try to go over a bridge to get to the house, but the river had flooded the bridge earlier in the day, and access was closed. Me and Brendan jump the fence to go and have a look.

When we finally get there we go out for an evening stroll with our wine in our hands, and we see kangaroos up on the hills.

The next day we go to Sydney, where we meet up with Ben Abraham and stay with Mark Serrels (he's the guy at Kotaku Australia, giant Glasgow accent, not even slightly diminished over time). We go for a drink and walk across the Sydney Harbour Bridge.

Australia has this weird thing called 'Big Things', which are large novelty objects put by roadsides to make a point of interest. We stop at one point by the Big Banana, which is somewhat literal.

Brendan in the Big Banana

Eventually we get into Brisbane. It's much hillier than Melbourne, and less 'hip', but there's still a lot to see and do. I go to stay with Christy for a while. She has a lovely ground-floor flat next to a pool in a trendy part of Brisbane.

Christy sitting near a fake beach

Originally from Melbourne, Christy moved to Brisbane for a Digital Writing Residency and stayed. She is now a senior lecturer in Games at the SAE Creative Media Institute. She's probably the best all-rounder I've met, in terms of the fact that she can turn her hand to virtually anything. She was primarily interested in comedy and theatre in the beginning, and she's really a writer-designer-director. She has worked on award-winning pervasive games, film, digital and theatre projects.

Recent successes: she was granted Australia's first Digital Writing Residency at The Cube for her project Robot University, funded by the Australia Council for the Arts and QUT. Her audio-driven app AUTHENTIC IN ALL CAPS won the 2014 WA Premier's Book Award in the Digital Narrative category; she won the 2014 Australian Writers Guild award for Interactive Media. Recently, she has become a powerhouse.

Brisbane's fake beach

The most wonderful thing about Christy is that she seems settled, to know what she wants, and she is very certain about her role – to experiment and play. She shows me dungeon dice – some dice etched with strange layouts of dungeon rooms made for role-playing games. She has reams of card games and books on game theory. She plies me with fizzy wine and we watch *Fear and Loathing in Las Vegas*, because although I've read the book now (I read it halfway through my journey) I had never seen the film. It's somewhat disappointing for me, I think because there's not as much evidence of the masterful words, and Hunter S.

Thompson somehow becomes more of an obnoxious figure when you are faced with real images of his actual behaviour. We probably should have taken some drugs. Or perhaps HST was not the hero I was looking for.

Every time we end up speaking over the next few days, Christy mentions this thing she has been thinking about: the idea that she is enough. I look up to her, I think, because looking at her career it is hard not to believe that she doesn't have every kind of game figured out, or every kind of creative expression. But she seems to have had this realisation very recently, that to have a creative voice of your own, of your very own, is enough. You don't have to have a 'message'.

'It's a different way of approaching games,' Christy says. 'I realised I could still have myself, and I could still have my worldview, which can still potentially contribute to the change in the world just by making something. It doesn't have to have an intention to change to actually be a force for transformation.

'I've got such a short time on earth. I don't want my stuff to just disappear into stuff that you do when you're alive.'

Goldie said something similar, about how she at one time had wanted to make a text game in Twine about the experiences of POWs in Changi, something that her and her mother were working on, gathering research on together.

'Stories, or personal experiences, aren't just like one thing filled with key events,' she says. 'The subtlety of a real-life story or experience is where it might hold "value" or "significance" in art. I made one Changi game, in Twine, but it was so disjointed in time, and every few pages had an option to stop the interview you were conducting in case the storyteller was getting anxious thinking about what he was telling you about – which was what he remembered about coming home. I was treading on glass, even though these guys are mostly all dead now. Mum had collected the interviews during the nineties and given me permission to

Twine them up. I never did anything much with it, but it's a good example, I think. Maybe I don't want to trivialise something huge just by pointing at its glaring features and turning them into a predestined path.'

Not too long ago, Christy lost her mother and I ask her if that was part of changing her mind.

'Before and after,' she says. 'The rubber hit the road when my mum died. She's fifty-eight. She's suddenly dead. Life is really short. So I don't have long. It was an aneurysm. She wasn't ill or anything. I called her up on the day that she died, and said, "I'm coming to see you finally!" And I kept calling and I was like, "Why aren't you responding?" The weird thing was she kept telling my brother and me she was going to be dying soon. She told us for years that she would not make it to 2012. She said she'd die beforehand.'

Goldie had said of Christy's design work on Magister Ludi: 'Damn, that game came from her. It was like the biggest, most refreshing breath of air I'd ever had, and it got me so excited for the future, and just told me to keep fucking around with thoughts and ideas. Her skills are great, she's a great writer. I think she totally justified her idea.'

I ask Christy how she thought about the design of Magister Ludi. She talks about how it had to be an installation, but also about how she wanted to open something up, and have the game be inside, such as a desk. She thought of escape-the-room games.

She also talks about how she left a recent traumatic relationship behind and tells me that she is now on a salary, where before she wasn't in such a good financial situation.

'But I was still in the same headstate,' she says. 'And I knew that, because I was consciously changing my life to get away from it. I can tell an abuser from a mile away now. But I was still having lack of confidence, dependency on others. The things that got me in that situation were still around. I had a salary but I was still spending money on debts instead of for myself. Living in the same poverty mindset. That's when I realised that there's things I needed to do for myself. That I got me in that situation. And so I decided to do a game about how there are things that you don't really escape, there are things that are dependent on you. That's when I was looking at the escape-the-room genre. I was looking at the mechanics of the game and thinking if it's about emphasising your role, then it's not about solving the puzzle to get out. It's about being the person who creates the problem in the first place.'

Magister Ludi is a game on a touchpad inside a school desk. You know it is ostensibly about teaching, but by the end of the game it has become obvious that you are creating the rigid structure yourself, and then obeying it. At some point, when I was playing the game, I understood that I could leave the situation completely. That I could just escape the room.

*

Dungeon Dice

As I write about it now, there's a strange framework that appears, and it's something to do with noticing Christy's contentment with her role in life. Magister Ludi is the outcome of Christy's escaping her room, but I lay in bed that night while Christy slept on the couch, and I thought about how, actually, I had escaped many rooms in 2014. I first had escaped poverty. Then I had escaped the old systems of journalism. I had escaped my old personal life. I had escaped from thinking I was not good enough. I had escaped from having to obey other people's editorial decisions. I had escaped from having to care what other people thought. I escaped all of the arguments about what a game is and what it should be and what developers I should be covering. I just did what I wanted. And it was enough.

'I realised I am enough,' Christy said to me.

In January I would walk into a room at the National Museum of Scotland in Edinburgh, that city being where I began my career at Rockstar Games years and years ago, and sit on a panel with three other distinguished men, and know that I was enough.

*

Thank you to all my backers, all the people who have put me up, friends, strangers, developers, anyone who told me a story, my editor Alison Rae, illustrator of my soul Irene Koh, anyone who was kind to me (almost everyone I met – even the strangers of Paris who picked up my gloves for me when I left them on a banlieue train). Thank you! I made it. You made it possible and no one ever snapped at me once, though I was probably a burden. And thank you to Brendan and Helen, and to both of your families for letting me stay for Christmas, and congratulations on getting hitched just after I left. You did it! I did it. We did it together.

Epilogue

People asked me, often, why I'd started out writing this series. In the beginning it felt like failure was the reason – London, after all, was mine, and it owed me a living but had never given me one. A self-centred position, but one necessary for survival. Creative people need to be paid a decent wage for work. It turned out that the world beyond of London was going to provide that pay, though like many games I've played in my life it wasn't as easy or as fun as I'd first projected.

But throughout writing what would become this book, it became clear to me that I was just documenting how excited I was, and still am, to be witnessing cultural change in games through the development of games. Change that is as culturally significant as what happened within the walls of Andy Warhol's The Factory. And even I was, at first, sort of reluctant to make that comparison – these days no one works under one roof, and of course we don't all know each other or take the same influences. But what is real about that comparison is that we all know *of* each other, there is a momentum, and we all work under an internet roof, and it's hard to make games these days without being inspired by what another gamemaker is doing, or even by a conversation that a gamemaker is trying to have. There's not one place in the world, for example, that I went, that women gamemakers didn't mention Anna Anthropy's groundbreaking work as a reason they existed in game development, and Rami Ismail of Vlambeer came up several times as an inspirational figure. They both haunted my text, like unofficial muses, or absent parents.

There's a fierce passion in games people all over the world to bring alternatives to what games have been for so long: the preserve of quick, insubstantial attention, devoid of any address to our wider culture, a territory colonised by a skewed view of masculine values or a strange adherence to investigating incidental experiences of violence but never to ask *why it was so widespread*. All of these people wanted to make things that bent that tunnel vision out of shape. Fetishising newness was always part of games, but we forgot to pay attention to new ways of making games and new people making them somewhere along the way.

There were many hardships that transpired in games circles in 2014, and every part of me wanted to give up what seemed like a frivolous task in the face of them. But I think in time I understood that my personal place was providing the passionate advocacy that others were too exhausted or upset to provide, to point to people who were still making in spite of it all, to try to do things in spite of my misgivings or fears. I made a personal decision to make something instead of giving up (even though it is perfectly legitimate to do so). There are a lot of ways in which everything in games has to be improved, but that means there is room for people to help in any way that they can.

I went out of my way to find people making games that no one had ever spoken about before, or who were really taking personal risks, or who were not the usual focus of what has become a western-centric community. People talk a lot about diversity but they often only mean with regard to people living in the UK or US. Since I was so mobile I thought, why aren't we talking about developers in Malaysia? In Singapore? In Australia? Ian Gregory was already holding a middle finger up to anti-gay laws in Singapore by writing gay romance into Witching Hour games, Ojiro Fumoto was busy making a Spelunky-like for mobile though the Japanese 'indie community' has only just been born. People are quick to say women indies are hard to find, but the women I wrote about in this book far, far outnumbered the men. I covered two women in Australia, Christy and Goldie, who were completely different from each other but who made a game together and it was put in an exhibition. If I'd been a stronger person I would have done it for another year and gone to India, South Africa, Brazil, the Philippines. But I was only physically and psychologically strong enough for a year.

It was a lot of work, but I am proud of it, because it is a cross-section, not just of exciting work, but of the sheer determination of people from a very wide variety of backgrounds making things they and I believe in. It is a document of, in Karla Zimonja's words, 'a fucking agenda', and in Nina Freeman's words, it is a document of 'fuck you, this is real'.

All hyperlinks were preserved in text and are indicated by an underline to allow readers to search terms later if they wish.

I always think of games as a document of closeness, of responses. I think this book is the closest I will ever get to telling you, the reader: for me games are about closeness.

I got closer to games in 2014 than I have ever been. I looked games in the heart, and it was terrible and wonderful, and I couldn't give less of a shit about what kind of journalism it was *supposed* to be. It was the kind of journalism where you look at the consequences and costs of existing in a space, and you think fuck it. We have all given something to pull the future closer to us, some more than others, but we will all be remembered if we keep writing it down and sharing it.

If I were an investigative journalist, perhaps I would conclude with my findings. I think my findings are this: Never shut up. It brings us together.

Cara Ellison is a Scottish writer, game critic and video game narrative designer. She has written for *The Guardian, VICE, Kotaku, PC Gamer, Paste* magazine and the *New Statesman,* wrote the best-names column in the world, S.EXE, at Rock Paper Shotgun, and had a regular opinion at *Eurogamer.* She was also co-writer on Charlie Brooker's *How Videogames Changed the World* for Channel 4 Television in the UK. Her writing and game narrative work has been featured in *The New York Times* and *Wired*, and she was one of *The Guardian's* Top Ten Young People in Digital media 2014. Currently she lives in Edinburgh where she designs the narratives for video games.

www.caraellison.co.uk
@caraellison